Day by Day with God

May–August 2004

DAY BY DAY

WITH GOD

Bible Readings for Women

MAY–AUGUST 2004

Christina Press
BRF
Tunbridge Wells/Oxford

The Bible Reading Fellowship,
First Floor, Elsfield Hall, 15–17 Elsfield Way, Oxford OX2 8FG

First published in Great Britain 2004

ISBN 1 84101 288 2

Jacket design: JAC Design for Print, Crowborough

Trade representation in UK:
Lion Publishing plc, Mayfield House, 256 Banbury Road
Oxford OX2 7DH

Distributed in Australia by:
Willow Connection, PO Box 288, Brookvale, NSW 2100.
Tel: 02 9948 3957; Fax: 02 9948 8153;
E-mail: info@willowconnection.com.au

Distributed in New Zealand by:
Scripture Union Wholesale, PO Box 760, Wellington
Tel: 04 385 0421; Fax: 04 384 3990; E-mail: suwholesale@clear.net.nz

Distributed in South Africa by:
Struik Book Distributors, PO Box 193, Maitland 7405
Tel: 021 551 5900; Fax: 021 551 1124; E-mail: enquiries@struik.co.za

Acknowledgments
Scriptures from The New Revised Standard Version of the Bible,
Anglicized Edition, copyright © 1989, 1995 by the Division of
Christian Education of the National Council of the Churches of
Christ in the USA, used by permission. All rights reserved.

Scripture quotations taken from *The Holy Bible, New International
Version*, copyright © 1973, 1978, 1984 by International Bible Society.
Used by permission of Hodder & Stoughton Ltd. All rights reserved.
'NIV' is a registered trademark of International Bible Society. UK
trademark number 1448790.

Scripture quotations from THE MESSAGE. Copyright © by Eugene H.
Peterson 1993, 1994, 1995. Used by permission of NavPress
Publishing.

Scripture quotations marked (NLT) are taken from the Holy Bible,
New Living Translation, copyright © 1996. Used by permission of
Tyndale House Publishers, Inc., Wheaton, Illinois 60189. All rights
reserved.

Printed in Great Britain by Bookmarque, Croydon

Contents

The Editor writes...

What an amazing promise Jesus has made: 'You will receive power when the Holy Spirit comes on you; and you will be my witnesses in Jerusalem, and in all Judea and Samaria, and to the ends of the earth.' Moments later, he was taken up into heaven and his disciples were left to wait. Then God surprised them: 'Suddenly a sound like the blowing of a violent wind came from heaven and filled the whole house where they were sitting. They saw what seemed to be tongues of fire that separated and came to rest on each of them. All of them were filled with the Holy Spirit' (Acts 2:2–4).

Pentecost, 30 May, is the time to celebrate this birthday of the Church—that long-promised moment when God poured his power into ordinary people like us. When Ezekiel prophesied about this turning point in history, he described a vast army: God's breath entered a collection of dry bones; they came to life and stood up on their feet.

Sometimes the Bible can seem like dry bones. We can read it intellectually and agree that it gives good guidelines for living. We can study its structure and language; it is a remarkable piece of literature, which is woven into the fabric of our culture. But Jesus fleshes out the Bible's words, first in his own body and then by giving us his Spirit to write God's words on our hearts. God's word and his Spirit go together—sometimes with surprising and unpredictable results.

As I write, Christians around the world are mourning the death of Bill Bright, who, with his wife Vonette, founded Campus Crusade for Christ International. Bill Bright was so motivated by the great commission that he wrote a four-point booklet on how to have a personal relationship with Jesus. This simple tract has been printed in some 200 languages and distributed to more than 2.5 billion people. Millions of people's lives have been transformed because Bill's booklet introduced them to Jesus. When Bill and Vonette left their sweet-making business in the 1950s to begin work with college students in California, they had no idea how our surprising God would use their work to reach the ends of the earth.

Bill and Vonette's story is remarkable, but not unique. Christian history is full of stories about ordinary people who've given their lives to God; as a result they have had the impact of a vast army.

Over these next four months, ask God to breathe his life into the words of the Bible as you read it each day. Look out for the different aspects of God that are revealed—the powerful God who created us and who surprises us by becoming a servant; the never-alone Trinity who is reflected in community. Look out for God at work through the ordinary stuff of life as he reveals himself and the extraordinary future he has in store for those who believe in him. Take time out in August to develop a deeper relationship with him, by using Christine Claydon's notes on contemplative prayer.

Whatever you hope to achieve between May and August this year, remember Jesus' words to Martha when Mary sat listening at his feet: 'You are worried and upset about many things, but only one thing is needed. Mary has chosen what is better' (Luke 10:41–42).

As you make time to focus on God, may he nourish your spirit with his words of life.

Catherine Butcher

7

Contributors

Fiona Barnard lives in Scotland. As staff member of Friends International, her principal work is among international students and researchers, encouraging local Christians to reach out in friendship to those temporarily far from home. She also teaches English to speakers of other languages on behalf of the local council.

Wendy Bray is a freelance writer, journalist and speaker with a special interest in family and relationship issues, and lives in Plymouth, Devon with her husband and two teenage children. She has a passion for flying, music, books and her friends and family. She is still waiting to fulfil her long-held ambition of flying with the Red Arrows.

Catherine Butcher took over from Mary Reid as editor of *Day by Day with God*. She is a freelance writer, publisher of *The Christian Counsellor* and consultant to *Woman Alive* magazine. Her first children's book, *Daniel & the Dark Arts*, was written under the pseudonym Earnest Spellbinder. She lives in Sussex with her husband and two school-age children.

Christine Claydon is a former RE teacher and vicar's wife. She lived in Israel for seven years, where she developed a contemplative prayer life through teaching, leading retreats and writing two books on the subject. Now back in Britain, she is a lay reader and helps lead others to develop a listening prayer life of their own.

Margaret Killingray is a tutor at the London Institute for Contemporary Christianity. She has assisted Dr John Stott and others in running Christian Impact conferences here and overseas. She and her husband live in Kent and have three daughters and five grandchildren.

Chris Leonard is married with two young-adult offspring. She has a degree in English and theology and her thirteen books range from biography and devotional to children's stories. She enjoys leading creative writing workshops because 'people are so interesting—and they grow!' Recent BRF publications include *The Heart of Christmas* and *The Road to Easter* (co-written with Jacqui Gardner).

Elaine Pountney, a pastoral counsellor and valued speaker, works for InterVarsity Canada, and is seconded to the former Soviet Union where she works part of the year in leadership development and formation of young Christian leaders. When in Canada, she delights in insightful interactions with her granddaughters, writing, and quiet walks on Pacific beaches marvelling at God's grace and mercy.

Wendy Pritchard is married to John, Bishop of Jarrow. She is a learning support assistant at a church secondary school, and mother of two daughters—one now married. Wendy has enjoyed each different phase of her life, from vicar's wife and maths teacher to mass caterer. She is interested in gardening, computing and solving life's problems.

Elizabeth Rundle is a Methodist minister, living in London. She has written books of daily readings, Bible studies and articles, and has contributed to regional religious programmes for both radio and television. She has led church weekends, women's conferences and pilgrimages to the Holy Land. In her dreams she would like to trot in the London Marathon!

Alie Stibbe is a freelance writer and translator who contributes regularly to Christian magazines. Her recent work includes *Word Bytes* (BRF 2003), 365 devotional readings for teenagers, translated from Norwegian. She has just embarked on a PhD in Scandinavian Studies, focusing on the devotional literature of the late 18th century Norwegian revival. Alie is married to Mark Stibbe, Vicar of St Andrew's Chorleywood. They have four children aged 6–14.

Sandra Wheatley lives in County Durham, is a qualified nurse and was diagnosed with multiple sclerosis fifteen years ago. She is single, lives alone, but is not lonely as family and friends live nearby. She has a variety of interests which keep her actively involved in the lives of those around her.

**Contributors are identified by their initials
at the bottom of each page.**

A Morning Prayer

Thank you, heavenly Father,
for this new day.
Be with me now
in all I do
and think
and say,
that it will be to your glory.

Amen

Double standards

To the pure, all things are pure.

Purity has become an unknown phenomenon, if our newspapers are to be believed. The press delight in uncovering the mixed motives and misplaced passions of people in high places. Leaders in politics and the Church are their favourite targets. As a journalist, I was trained to uncover corruption and report on wrongdoing. The press are criticized when they expose the private lives of public figures. But often, that's what they should be doing. The public expects integrity, especially in leaders. Private vices have an impact on public life.

However, the media can have double standards. Paul's letter to Titus grates against modern political correctness. The qualities it espouses feature in the media caricature of a Christian—serious, temperate, humble, busy, 'eager to do what is good'. You can imagine the slightly built, sandal-wearing priest or the teetotaller busybody in a TV sitcom. The press call for purity, but ridicule those who put God's principles into practice. And woe betide anyone who says God's plan for living has boundaries and no-go areas. Satan still whispers that forbidden fruit is 'good, pleasing and desirable' (Genesis 3:6) and fruitless debates follow about how far we can go across God's boundary lines.

Paul's letter to Titus offends modern sensibilities—even those in the Church. His advice to women doesn't seem to fit with modern trends. His expectations of leaders seem impossibly high. Is Paul's advice simply out of date? How should we behave as Christian women? What should we expect of our leaders in the Church?

Crete, where Titus worked, was known for laziness, gluttony, lying and evil. The Greek world around AD64, when Paul wrote this pastoral letter, had many similarities with today's Western world. Over the next few days, we will be looking at Titus to find out how we should live, and how the good citizenship guidelines in this letter square with a God who welcomes wayward prodigals with a passionate Father's embrace.

Ask God to help you to hear his voice rather than the noisy claims of modern culture on how you should live.

CB

Blameless leaders

*Since an overseer is entrusted with God's work, he must be
blameless—not overbearing, not quick-tempered, not given to
drunkenness, not violent, not pursuing dishonest gain.*

One of the perks of a journalist's job is going backstage to interview a
platform party, band or performers in a more private setting. When
the spotlight's turned off, some famous names lose their lustre. When
the grease paint washes off, ugliness can be more than skin deep.

In 1986 I helped run the press office at a conference, which
included dozens of national and international 'names' from the
Christian world. Millions had read their books or heard them preach.
Some of those leaders stand out in my memory to this day because
they were so gracious and considerate, humble and kind, even under
pressure.

When Paul sent his list of leaders' qualities to Titus, he didn't
include public charisma, educational qualifications or preaching style.
He *did* focus on relationships and home life. Being hospitable and
bringing up well-behaved children were more important than the
ability to hold an audience's attention. As Paul says in a similar
job-description sent to Timothy: 'If anyone does not know how to
manage his own family, how can he take care of God's church?'
(1 Timothy 3:5).

Church leaders have to balance work, rest and recreation. Caring
for our own families can be a training—and testing—ground for
Christian leadership. Paul puts the onus on leaders to be blameless,
resisting the temptations of money, sex and power. Again, these are
skills learned at home before leaders are launched into a pubic arena.

But it's sad when a godly leader's greatest adversaries are sitting in
church week by week, waiting for Sunday lunch and roast preacher!
One wrong move and the critics in the congregation are ready to
pounce. Let's be people who love and support our leaders.

'Remember your leaders, who spoke the word of God to you. Consider
the outcome of their way of life and imitate their faith' (Hebrews
13:7). Pray for your church leaders today, praying particularly for
their children.

CB

Shiny lives

They claim to know God, but by their actions they deny him.

In the last census, 71 per cent of people in England and Wales said that they were Christians, but what proportion live out that claim with changed lives? How many even know how Jesus wants us to live?

This summer thousands of Christian young people will be in London for 'Soul in the City'. This Soul Survivor mission will include Christian teaching and worship, but the lasting message will be that loving God makes a difference to the way we live.

Christians will spend part of every day working on community projects. The way Christians speak and act towards each other speaks volumes. Also, by painting community centres, reclaiming parkland from rubbish or cleaning graffiti from a shopping parade, the mission will create a lasting legacy of physical change in communities, say the organizers.

As Titus shows, people's lives change when they become Christians. In the past, this has given rise to the Bible-belt phenomenon: people in inner cities become Christians, don't want to live surrounded by drunkenness, violence and dishonesty, so move to 'better' areas with 'nicer' schools and 'respectable' neighbours. The drunkenness, violence and dishonesty still goes on, though—it's just behind closed doors.

Over five years ago, a Manchester church sent a team to live on an inner-city estate. It's called the Eden Project and volunteer workers are committed to living long-term in the inner city, in full-time work or education, praying hard, being friends to young people and getting involved in the community as members of a strong local church. Lives are being changed as people see faith put into practice.

When Jesus came: 'The Word became flesh and blood, and moved into the neighbourhood. We saw the glory with our own eyes' (John 1:14, *THE MESSAGE*). Today, if the world is to see Jesus, it needs to see him in us, in our neighbourhood, living productive lives, which have been transformed by his love.

Father, help me to be transparent so your glory shines through me today.
CB

Models and maturity

*... teach the older women... Then they can train
the younger women to love their husbands and children...*

One of the anecdotes to emerge after the Queen Mother died,
revealed her sense of humour. After seeing the controversial comic
Ali G on TV, she learned to mimic his actions. One day after lunch
she stood up, clicked her fingers the way Ali G does, and said to the
Queen: 'Darling, lunch was marvellous—respec!'

Respect has become a comedian's catchphrase, but it's often a
missing ingredient in modern homes. The apostle Paul had a keen
insight into our emotional needs. When he told husbands to love
their wives as Christ loves the Church, 'giving himself up for her'
(Ephesians 5:25–33), he said, 'the wife must respect her husband'.
Although we all crave love and respect, in general, the need for
respect is higher on a man's list. When feminism rocked the postwar
balance of relationships, respect for men was a major casualty.

Women who prickle at the prospect of putting these words of
Paul into practice, need to heed his gender-neutral challenge:
'Submit to one another out of reverence for Christ' (Ephesians
5:21). The Saviour we serve 'made himself nothing, taking the very
nature of a servant... he humbled himself and became obedient to
death' (Philippians 2:7, 8). That is not a mandate for wife-beaters.
It is a challenge to both men and women to follow our servant-mas-
ter. As Jesus said, to be great, we must be servants (Matthew 20:26).

Titus gives us a photo-fit picture of a model of godly goodness. It
is not unlike the Proverbs 31 woman: 'She watches over the affairs
of her household and does not eat the bread of idleness'. 'Her husband is respected...'

Do you know women who are models of goodness? Who are your
role models and what are you modelling for younger women? Are
you sometimes outwardly respectful, but silently disparaging of men
in your circle?

---

*Jesus, thank you for setting the standard for greatness with a life of
service and obedience. Show me how to follow your lead today and
give me a submissive heart.*

CB

Too good to be true

For the grace of God that brings salvation has appeared to all...

Little Goody Two Shoes is one of the oldest published children's stories, about an orphan girl with only one shoe. She was nicknamed Goody Two Shoes when a shoemaker gave her a pair of new shoes and she was delighted, but now the nickname is given to self-righteous, smugly virtuous people.

On first reading, the godly character traits described in Titus can create this 'Goody Two Shoes' image. This trustworthy, self-controlled, pure person who is eager to do good, seems too perfect to be possible.

Perversely the world seems to despise people who live upright, godly lives. Workers who try to please their employers (Titus 2:9) are ridiculed by colleagues. Even Jesus seemed harsh about Goody Two Shoes types: he said the religious leaders of the day were 'like manicured grave plots... but six feet down it's all rotting bones and worm-eaten flesh. People look at you and think you're saints, but beneath the skin you're total frauds' (Matthew 23:27, 28, THE MESSAGE).

People look at outward appearances, but God looks at our hearts. He isn't impressed by Mrs Bucket ('Bouquet') characters keeping up appearances to impress the neighbours. He'd rather keep the company of tax collectors and notorious sinners; at least they are real.

The grace of God is the key to Christian character. Even the best-behaved Goody Two Shoes doesn't make the grade with God—none of us can achieve his standards ourselves—but Jesus' death makes us acceptable to God. 'Saving is all his idea, and all his work... It's God's gift from start to finish! We don't play the major role. If we did, we'd probably go around bragging that we'd done the whole thing!' (Ephesians 2:8, 9, THE MESSAGE)

Our lives change in response to his love. God's grace teaches us how to live godly lives.

'Twas grace that taught my heart to fear,
And grace my fears relieved;
How precious did that grace appear
The hour I first believed.
JOHN NEWTON 1779

CB

Power source

At one time, we too were foolish, disobedient, deceived and enslaved by all kinds of passions and pleasures. We lived in malice and envy, being hated and hating one another.

Do you remember the ugly sisters in Cinderella? They're foolish, selfish, malicious and envious—just like the people Paul describes. Imagine how indignant we would feel if one of them was transformed into the beautiful bride who stole Prince Charming's heart. Although Cinderella's clothes are in tatters, we reckon her heart is good. She deserves to become the prince's true love.

In God's amazing salvation plans, however, the ones who become his heirs were once the ugly sisters. As Paul explained to the Ephesians, 'because of his great love for us, God, who is rich in mercy, made us alive with Christ even when we were dead in transgressions—it is by grace you have been saved' (2:4–5).

The Christian manifesto for a better society does not include a self-improvement programme. Corrupt societies are transformed when people are introduced to the love and mercy of God. Handed over to him, we are washed clean, reborn into his family and renewed by his Holy Spirit who comes to live in us to guide us. We can make a fresh start. Instead of being condemned as failures, we are 'justified'—God treats us 'just as if' we've never sinned. That's what grace does—as the mnemonic goes, grace is God's Riches At Christ's Expense. God has done all the work. Like an ugly-sister-Cinderella, we are transformed from the inside. He moves us from the kingdom of darkness into his kingdom of light. As heirs instead of slaves, we become part of God's royal family. Our behaviour changes *as a result of* the changes God has made first.

Trust in the Lord and do good; dwell in the land and enjoy safe pasture. Delight yourself in the Lord and he will give you the desires of your heart. Commit your way to the Lord; trust in him and he will do this: He will make your righteousness shine like the dawn...
PSALM 37:3–6

CB

Productive living

… avoid foolish controversies and genealogies and arguments and quarrels about the law, because these are unprofitable and useless.

A few years ago I was part of an informal group of Christians from different churches, working together to share God's love in the community. Its diversity was remarkable. No one had decided to form a church unity committee, but we loved God, longed to see his love shared throughout the community and respected each other's different expressions of Christian faith. It was as if God had joined hearts together: like Margaret Thatcher and Mikail Gorbachev, we were very different, but we knew we could do business together.

Then one dear Christian man decided the town's churches needed something more formal, tied down to a Basis of Faith to ensure we all believed the same things, to the letter. The group evaporated like invisible ink as the formal alliance began.

Living by a written code seems neater and easier. It means I don't have to build a relationship with a fellow Christian, before I can agree to work alongside him or her; the piece of paper says we both believe the same things, so we must be compatible. But, 'the letter kills… the Spirit gives life' (2 Corinthians 3:6).

Paul wanted Titus' work in Crete to be profitable. Through these three short chapters he set out clear priorities: appoint strong, blameless leaders who teach sound doctrine; encourage godly living through right relationships in the church, at home and in the workplace; stress God's grace as the source of right living; and finally, stay focused—avoid arguments and have nothing to do with divisive people.

Do you waste endless energy on pointless arguments? What gets you fired up—church decor and music; details of church practice and style; or how to help the people you meet daily to find the hope Jesus offers? What's your focus?

'Walk—better yet, run!—on the road God called you to travel… steadily, pouring yourselves out for each other in acts of love, alert at noticing differences and quick at mending fences' (Ephesians 4:1–6, THE MESSAGE).

CB

Living God's way

Grace be with you all!

Today we return to the heart of Paul's letter to Titus: the transformation that God does when he saves us. Look at the contrast: foolish, disobedient, malicious, envious people, full of hatred, enslaved by all kinds of passions and pleasures. Then God steps in: 'He gave us a good bath, and we came out of it new people, washed inside and out by the Holy Spirit. Our Saviour Jesus poured out new life so generously. God's gift has restored our relationship with him and given us back our lives. And there's more life to come—an eternity of life!' (Titus 3:5–7, THE MESSAGE).

The rest of Titus shows the impact of such a transformation: leaders who are hospitable, self-controlled, upright, holy and disciplined with godly family lives; wise older men who are worthy of respect, sound in faith, love and endurance, who teach younger men by their good example; reverent older women who encourage younger women to be loving and kind, with well-run homes; loyal employees who can be relied on for their integrity.

Political correctness might make Titus seem difficult to swallow whole, but which society do you prefer: the corrupt society where liars, evil brutes and lazy gluttons have their way or one where God's grace has transformed men and women from the inside out. It is not a question of lawlessness versus good government. Good laws can help, but our lives need to be changed by God's grace. Then, with his Holy Spirit as a constant companion and guide, our lives become radically different. We put Jesus' teaching into practice, because we are grateful for his amazing love.

The world is watching. They are not interested in empty words, they want to see if faith makes a difference to friendships, marriages, parenting, home life and the wider world. People haven't changed much since Titus' day. Many still want a fresh start, new strength for today and hope for the future.

'Let your light shine before men, that they may see your good deeds and praise your Father in heaven' (Matthew 5:16).

CB

Cities of refuge

… set aside for yourselves… cities centrally located in the land the Lord your God is giving you to possess. Build roads to them…, so that anyone who kills a man may flee there.

I was intrigued when a woman visiting our church said she saw it as a 'city of refuge'. Searching the scriptures, I was surprised to find many references to these cities, but knew very little about them. What were they? How might a church be like them?

It turned out that these six designated 'cities of refuge' in the promised land provided asylum for people who committed manslaughter, rather than murder. 'If he had unintentionally killed his neighbour without malice aforethought he could flee into one of these cities and save his life' (Deuteronomy 4:42). Good practical stuff, but we have sophisticated justice systems designed to cope with such things today. Is this still important? And, gulp, why would we want our nice, newly decorated church full of maybe-murderers?

When our children were small, we stayed in a guest house. The owners had been so impacted by the experience of a previous couple of guests, that they themselves needed to talk endlessly about it. The male guest had, through some dreadful accident, run over his two-year-old son in his own front drive. Imagine. How horrific!

Most of us will not have killed anyone, accidentally or otherwise. Yet, with fatal traffic smashes running at record levels (even where no dangerous driving occurred), with medical staff having to make fine decisions that can result in death, with parents' agonies over cot-death or teenage meningitis deaths, many of us will know someone haunted by a largely innocent, unpunishable 'guilt'. And that's without mentioning legal, but lethal, abortions. Surely a church is somewhere such people should be able to find forgiveness, cleansing, deliverance from horror and a new life in Jesus.

Do our churches know how to deal with these things? Do we provide refuges or irrelevancies?

Thank you, Father, for forgiveness. Thank you for the fresh start we can have because of Jesus.

CL

Crime...

Do not pollute the land where you are. Bloodshed pollutes the land, and atonement cannot be made for the land on which blood has been shed, except by the blood of the one who shed it. Do not defile the land where you live and where I dwell, for I, the Lord, dwell among the Israelites.

When someone is killed, we are shocked—and God is even more concerned. When the first murder happened, as described in the fourth chapter of Genesis, God himself brought judgment, then said, 'From each man, too, I will demand an accounting for the life of his fellow man. "Whoever sheds the blood of man, by man shall his blood be shed; for in the image of God has God made man"' (Genesis 9:5–6).

We have to understand this background if we are going to understand cities of refuge. People belong to God; made in his image, but not licensed to kill. The land is God's—especially the promised land, where he intended his rule to prevail, as his chosen people lived as a light to the nations. Killing defiled and polluted it. We are not so different. Think of Hungerford, Lockerbie, Dunblane, Enniskillin—and what these small-town names mean to us now.

If our Father God takes killing extremely seriously, Jesus implied that anyone who is angry 'with his brother' will be subject to the same judgment (Matthew 5:21–22). It makes sense. Have you ever been at a party or family meal where there has been a big row? That too pollutes the atmosphere, drives away the Spirit of God and makes earth less like his kingdom.

Atonement (at-one-ment) comes through Jesus who shed his own blood, to heal, to purify, to restore our relationship with God and with one another

---

Thank you, Father God, that you embrace something far deeper than Numbers 35 or Genesis 9. Thank you that full atonement is made, not by a guilty person, but by someone entirely innocent, even of sin in thought. Thank you, Jesus, for becoming a city of refuge for all of us.

CL

... and punishment

Christ... entered the Most Holy Place once for all by his own blood... without the shedding of blood there is no forgiveness.

Imagine a time long ago, before policemen or an established rule of law. Imagine, not a nation state, but loosely associated tribes, each made up of extended family groupings or 'clans'. If someone robbed or killed someone in your clan, all of you suffered. So someone, usually the nearest male member of the family, would have to avenge the wrong, by killing the murderer—that was justice. If the murder was an accident, people might well feel that this was unfair—and appoint someone to murder him. Soon there was a full-scale blood feud. This was where cities of refuge came into their own.

This 'avenger of blood' was known, in Hebrew, as the '*go-el*' and he had other jobs to do on behalf of near relations. If you got into debt and were forced to sell your land, or even to sell yourself into slavery, your nearest male relative (your *go-el*) would have first option to buy. He would effectively redeem you and/or your land, so that neither passed away from the clan.

Exploring these ancient customs left me excited because of the light they shed on our inheritance as Christians. Jesus is our Redeemer, the payer of our debts. Just as Yahweh-God served as *go-el* to his people Israel, delivering them from slavery in Egypt, so Jesus delivers us from slavery to sin, self, addiction, fear... from slavery to any number of things. Adopting us as siblings, he makes us a community living under grace. This unique *go-el*, who paid our blood-debt with his own life, is also our avenger. We have no need to 'get even' with those who have wronged us, or become consumed by hatred, bitterness and desire for revenge. We can let go and trust in him to judge both them and us.

My Redeemer, my Refuge, my Justice, my Brother, my Saviour, my Deliverer, my Forgiveness, my Avenger... by which name will you worship Jesus today?

CL

How did cities of refuge work?

... the assembly must judge between [one who kills
unintentionally] and the avenger of blood according to these
regulations... must protect the... accused... from the avenger of
blood and send him back to the city of refuge to which he fled. He
must stay there until the death of the high priest.

Do read the whole chapter, letting it paint the full picture. In summary, though, if you killed someone and reached a city of refuge before his *go-el* caught you, the city elders would hold you under their protection until you could be judged, most likely at the scene of the crime, before any witnesses. If found guilty of murder, you would be handed over to the *go-el*. If it was judged that you had not intended to kill, you would receive safe passage back to the city of refuge—but if you left it before the death of the high priest, you would no longer come under its protection.

The cities, six in all, were well spread, for ease of access, and were among 48 cities ceded to the Levites. Unlike the other tribes, Levites were not given whole regions of the promised land but only about 16 square miles comprising these cities and their surrounding pastures. They would undertake their temple duties by rota and spend the rest of the year in their own cities.

All very interesting—but how does it apply to us? Well, the Levites were a tribe of priests and we are a 'kingdom of priests'. How fascinating that those who are most involved in worship and prayer are also charged with being passionate about justice! Worship, compassion and justice must be marks of any community dedicated to our God—and Jesus is our High Priest.

We don't know how much city of refuge law was actually put into practice, but we can thank God for his care for details and for the symbolism that speaks to us down the ages.

Father God, give me a heart of compassion. Show me where to take
a stand for justice.

CL

The bride of Christ

Husbands, love your wives, just as Christ loved the church and gave himself up for her to make her holy, cleansing her by the washing with water through the word, and to present her to himself as a radiant church, without stain or wrinkle or any other blemish, but holy and blameless.

What else might we learn from the teaching about cities of refuge? Was our visitor right in believing that churches today could learn from or be like them? What are the marks of a true church, anyway? I am going to consider these questions by looking at the different New Testament 'pictures' of a true church—temple, bride, family, vine and so on—asking how each picture might relate to cities of refuge.

First, there's the church as the pure bride of Christ—not much room for guilt-ridden killers here, surely! Except that, if Jesus is cleansing his bride, she must be dirty. Who is more radiant than a once-filthy person emerging from a long, hot, fragrant bath? Those receiving real forgiveness are radiant with love—as Jesus said of the 'sinful woman' who wiped his feet with her hair, 'Her many sins have been forgiven—for she loved much. But he who has been forgiven little loves little' (Luke 7:47).

There will be pain, of course—for Jesus and for the church. As I write, our local paper has the headline, 'Homeless man helped by church group admits to shoplifting'. A church in a nearby town got talking to him, found him accommodation and work—then, already out on a conditional discharge, he couldn't resist another petty crime spree. It cost—bad publicity for the church perhaps—but he is off drugs, and, in time, as the grace of Jesus and of Christians work their cleansing transformation, he may be filled with pure joy.

Jesus, I'm so grateful that you cleanse me—I need that every day. Cleanse all of us guilty ones who, living in your 'city of refuge', are becoming your bride.

                                                                    CL

The vine

I am the vine; you are the branches. If a man remains in me and I in him, he will bear much fruit.

None of us change overnight, do we? We need time, just as a vine needs time to grow. We grow and change as Christians by letting Christ's life flow through us as constantly as our own life-blood does, but this passage doesn't apply to individuals as much as to communities, to churches. We each have our place on a branch or twig. Jesus' life flows to us through others, very often.

So what about people on the edge, people who are not attached to the vine yet? Well, surely if killers were sheltering long-term in cities of refuge under the protection of priests or Levites, many must have become absorbed in the city's worship and life. The same could apply to those who drift within our orbit. I don't only mean those who attend church, but anyone to whom the life, care, love and prayer of a church-person flows. That is a lot of people. Some will become grafted on. They might tear themselves off again but, given time, and love, they might become a true part of the vine, the city.

To take a small example, an individual who came occasionally to our church was caught more than once pilfering silverware from the Tearcraft stall. 'Years later I had the privilege of praying with him as he declared where the Lord was in his life,' said a church member with joint responsibility for the stall. 'There was pain—but then such joy!'

Are we big enough to include people who need time and space? People going through marriage difficulties or divorce, nervous breakdowns, people who have bad attitudes, kids who have gone wrong, outcasts… reaching out from our particular 'twig' of the vine, can we allow Jesus' life to flow in the direction of one or two of these? It will cost us, in time if nothing else. Ask Jesus—and remember that he is your enabler.
CL

Temple—a worshipping city

... built on the foundation of the apostles and prophets, with Christ Jesus himself as the chief cornerstone. In him the whole building is joined together and rises to become a holy temple in the Lord. And in him you too are being built together to become a dwelling in which God lives by his Spirit.

'I can't wait to go to church on Sunday mornings,' said a friend recently. 'I know I'm loved and accepted there—and somehow I can breathe again after all the troubles of the week. It's partly the worship. The music isn't always exactly as I like it but there's something about worshipping God together with people I love. I can't describe why it lifts me so much!'

We had been praying about her friend's husband's redundancy and over her own worries about a teenage daughter and ageing mother—and praising God too. 'I feel all warm,' she said afterwards, 'as though God's giving me a big hug!' Feelings aren't everything, but they can help!

A temple is for worship—which isn't just singing and praying but about living our lives to please God as we're joined in harmony with one another. Any church that is built true has to give Jesus the most important place—he is the cornerstone. There is something extraordinarily healing about being 'templed' with people who live in wonder at God's goodness and love, who exist not to please themselves but to please him and to love one another. I don't think it's by chance that the cities of refuge, belonging as they did to the priest-Levites, were worshipping communities.

Lord, I couldn't count the number of times you have healed and restored me as I've worshipped you—whether that worship consisted of doing what you said or being 'lost in wonder, love and praise'. Thank you for who you are, for the refuge we find when we meet you in worship and for our fellow worshippers, who are joined to us because they are joined to you.

CL

Family refuge

… my brothers, you whom I love and long for, my joy and crown… stand firm in the Lord, dear friends! I plead with Euodia and I plead with Syntyche to agree with each other in the Lord… help these women who have contended at my side in the cause of the gospel.

Families—those without them are bereft. Yet family life can often feel more like a battleground than a refuge. And it's no different in the Church. The New Testament is full of references to us as God's family. We are his sons and daughters. We are Jesus' (and therefore each others') sisters and brothers. New Testament letters are written to 'Brothers' (normally meaning sisters too.) But early church leaders were realists. Sisters squabble—but they are still sisters. They are still part of the family of God, which has a responsibility to help restore right relations between them.

These days many people live far from their wider family—and, as the pace of life quickens, may not even know their neighbours. Communities are breaking down, leaving huge holes for individuals to fall down. The church family is in prime position to prove a very real refuge to desperate people, but not if it is dysfunctional. Not if the quarrels of today's Euodias and Syntyches are allowed to fester and spread to poison family life. Sometimes everything seems friendly, but the paper is barely covering the cracks, but real community, real family, is where people have time and commitment for one another. Then it's a joy and a crown for the King—and a demonstration of his holy city, his kingdom.

A father to the fatherless, a defender of widows… God sets the lonely in families (Psalm 68:5–6) The King will reply, 'I tell you the truth, whatever you did for one of the least of these brothers of mine, you did for me' (Matthew 25:40). As we have opportunity, let us do good to all people, especially to those who belong to the family of believers (Galatians 6:10).

CL

The flock finds refuge

Keep watch over yourselves and all the flock of which the Holy Spirit has made you overseers. Be shepherds of the church of God, which he bought with his own blood.

Paul is on his way to Jerusalem, talking to the elders of the Ephesian church where he laboured so hard and long, and is sad because he knows, 'that none of you among whom I have gone about preaching the kingdom will ever see me again'.

John 10 tells us we are all lost sheep, found by the good shepherd, who laid down his life for us. He became the gate by which we enter the safe refuge of the sheepfold, but Paul knows that 'there are still savage wolves [which] will come in among you and will not spare the flock'. Bereft of Paul, the elders of the church have a duty to watch over the flock, protecting it—perhaps even from wolves in sheep's clothing.

A church, city, or sheepfold needs to be a safe refuge where those at the end of their tether—the young, the weak, damaged or vulnerable—can find security for healing, growth, cleansing…

Jesus attracted some unsavoury types when he walked this earth, though. What if we welcome the kind of people he did? What if our churches attract repentant alcoholics who lapse occasionally into drunken violence? Or paedophiles, released from prison, hoping desperately that Jesus will give them power to change—because who else will accept them?

We need to pray for supernatural wisdom for our leaders, because a refuge cannot be allowed to become a place of danger. People with such desperate needs, along with those with chronic physical or mental problems, can put a huge strain on those caring for them. An individual or nuclear family might go under. Better a group, drawing on the skills, wisdom, prayer and time of many.

Thank you, Jesus, for saying, 'Do not be afraid, little flock, for your Father has been pleased to give you the kingdom' (Luke 12:32).

CL

Called out for a purpose

*You are Peter, a rock. This is the rock on which I will put together
my church, a church so expansive with energy that not even the
gates of hell will be able to keep it out.*

'Church' (*ecclesia* in Greek) means 'called out ones'. Not a religious
word, it describes a group of people 'called out' for a specific purpose—for example to defend the city against attack, to judge something or to build something. A purposeless *ecclesia* makes no sense.
God didn't call us for holy huddles, but as his tool to win back his
kingdom. He has equipped us to attack the very gates of hell,
promising they would fall. (The NIV version says 'the gates of Hades
will not overcome it': Sorry, NIV—the meaning here is not unsuc-
cessful attacks by the gates of hell, but the church on the attack,
smashing those gates to smithereens.)

Does the thought of yourself, your church or an impulsive fisher-
man called Simon Peter and his mates overcoming hell seem just
too improbable? If you know the book or film, think of that scene in
Tolkien's *Lord of the Rings* where halflings Frodo and Sam cower
before the terrifying gates of the hellish kingdom of Mordor. They
prevail finally because their enemy cannot conceive of anyone being
willing to sacrifice themselves in the face of such power.

In a battle there are many small things to do. Regular 'ecclesias'
maintained the roads that led to the cities of refuge—and ensured
the signposting remained clear. We are to do the same. We need
church-based people, praying and caring for those already there. As
our visitor said to our church, though, we also need 'runners' who
will go out and encourage those who are making their way to the
city and we need watchers on the walls who will send up flares,
showing our position to those who have lost their way—that they
may be 'reclaimed, recovered and redeemed'.

---

*Praise God that he is making himself known 'in the heavenly realms'
(Ephesians 3:10). Ask God to underline his purpose for you today.*

CL

Salt and light

You are the light of the world. A city on a hill cannot be hidden.

I am picturing the ancient hill towns in Galilee, their lights twinkling a welcome from the dark and dangerous night. It is lovely to think of Jesus as the light of the world, too, but when I start thinking of the church in the same role... gulp! Surely Jesus didn't mean people like me?! Yes, he did. He goes on to say, 'let your light shine before men, that they may see your good deeds and praise your Father in heaven'.

Too often in history churches have been known for their hatred, although some good deeds shine bright—for example the good work done by the Salvation Army is sometimes acknowledged in today's media. But the light from a city comes from many sources within it, both powerful and faint. Think of your church and all the little kindnesses that happen, day by day. You won't know about most of them, but God does—and sees his kingdom advancing.

Very occasionally more people get to see the light shining from 'ordinary' Christians. As I write, news programmes have been scrutinizing the life of a special branch policeman fatally stabbed by terrorists—and praising his goodness and compassion towards his family, church, work and community.

We are to be salt, too—enhancing taste, preventing rot in food. My daughter, about to study English literature at university, worried how little she knew of Greek and Roman legends—until some English graduates said, 'Actually, the Bible's far more use, since most of the renowned writers you'll study were Christians.' It's true! Think of Christians who work in medicine, education, social services, the arts, the law—anywhere really. Where would our world be without them?

Pray, that the light of Jesus shining in us may be effective in attracting people to enter his kingdom. Pray for everyone promoting goodness and justice in this world in God's name, that we won't allow God-given salt to lose its potency.

CL

Body with open arms

... in Christ we who are many form one body... We have different gifts, according to the grace given us.

'O fount of all knowledge, why is a tank full of invisible fish bubbling away in the church lobby?' I asked Margery, as she sat behind the welcome desk on Sunday morning.

'Oh, it's for the children—they're studying animals at the church playschool and someone's bringing fish for the tank tomorrow.'

I voiced relief that our church wasn't installing a dental surgery upstairs. Margery confessed her disappointment that the tank had not been used to house fresh fish for cooking on the health and hygiene course the day before. 'Official inspectors insist all who use the church kitchen must be certificated, but I only go there to wash up,' she laughed. A retired special needs teacher, Margery helps our church-and-community playschool, 'old people' and God knows how many others—she's loved by the whole village for her sense of humour and practical kindnesses.

We waved at our minister, just returned from two weeks in a war-torn country, using his highly specialized skills of post-traumatic stress debriefing. I thought how the church had functioned apparently stress-free in his absence and how, though we can always grumble about things going wrong, we do work together effectively. Last week I was 'volunteered' to take notes in a small meeting. Judith (not appreciating its illegibility) admired the speed of my writing so dejectedly that we all rounded on her. 'What about you, cooking gourmet Alpha suppers for 40 without a single flap?'

That's a quirky snapshot of part of one small, far from perfect 'body of Christ'. Its members often think themselves insignificant, but together they are providing a 'city of refuge' for the old, the young, the lost, the sad, even (at arm's stretch) the traumatized on the other side of the world. Those who help us satisfy official inspectors are vital, too!

Lord, help each of us to recognize our local expressions of your body and play our own parts, under your direction.

CL

Ultimate city of refuge

*By faith Abraham… obeyed and went… like a stranger in a
foreign country; he lived in tents… For he was looking forward to
the city with foundations, whose architect and builder is God.*

Are you a city or a country person at heart? I would far rather relax
in a garden or go for a nice country walk than push my way over
hard pavements through the noise, dirt and blank-faced crowds of a
sprawling, crime-filled metropolis. But, although the 'city of God'
isn't my favourite picture of the Church, I have to admit that a city
designed by and built upon God would be a marvel.

Unlike me, God is passionate about cities. That's just as well,
considering that most of the world's population live in them. Cities
form a major theme throughout the Bible, with cities of refuge being
a small sub-set. There are wicked cities, like Sodom, or the 'harlot'
Babylon. There are cities where men think they are in charge—
Babel, or James 4:13–14 which says, 'Now listen, you who say,
"Today or tomorrow we will go to this or that city, spend a year
there, carry on business and make money." Why, you do not even
know what will happen tomorrow.' These types of cities are all rec-
ognizable today.

Then there is Jerusalem, whose name means 'City of Peace'—
ironic, isn't it? Perhaps it was because God had such plans, made
such investment in that city, that it became a focus for contention.
The problem lay not so much with outside forces but with his own
people, who refused to walk in his ways, choosing rebellion rather
than his *shalom*—peace-wholeness. Do read Luke 19:41–44, where
Jesus wept over Jerusalem.

---

*Lord, of course you long for the multitudes you love to live in harmony
with yourself and one another. The only way that will happen is if the
architecture of our lives is founded on, designed and built by you.
Help us, in an individualistic age, to apply that to our churches.*

CL

Church as the heavenly city

But you have come to Mount Zion, to the heavenly Jerusalem, the city of the living God. You have come to thousands upon thousands of angels in joyful assembly, to the church of the firstborn, whose names are written in heaven.

Note the tense. It is the perfect: 'You *have* come'. So this is not future or conditional, it is not about 'pie in the sky when you die'— but do these extraordinarily inspiring words match reality? Church too often seems not so much a place of glory, or even refuge, more a place where people get hurt. That is all the more painful because our expectations are so high—of love, peace, acceptance, kindness, forgiveness, healing, never mind 'thousands of angels'.

The other day I was talking to a woman who, because of certain things that had happened, felt unwelcome and uneasy at her church. Having heard only one side of the story, I am unclear whether the main problem lay with others' actions or her reactions, but I found myself saying, 'Actually, whatever people say or do, you are welcome, in that the only reason anyone can be welcome in any church is because of Jesus.' We have all done things wrong, we have all hurt others and been hurt, we all keep falling far short of behaving like heavenly citizens.

This passage in Hebrews is contrasted to the harsher old covenant, where law-breakers lived in terror of God, but in heaven, Jesus writes for all eternity the names of all who love him, and welcomes them in this world to his table, to feast on his body and his blood. All Christians are equal there, none is excluded or unwelcome, all have a 'right' to be there. Only those who eat and drink 'without recognizing the body of the Lord' eat and drink judgment on themselves (1 Corinthians 11:29). Who is the body of the Lord? We are!

Thank you, Lord, that a true church is not only a refuge, but a city-wide party where angels celebrate, alongside humans, the extraordinary grace of God.

CL

Visions in exile and a call

... while I was among the exiles by the Kebar River, the heavens
were opened and I saw visions of God.

What a strange place and time to receive a vision! In exile; in captivity to a foreign power. Do you ever wonder why God's voice sounds so strong when we are in exile? Removed and isolated from the comfort of the familiar or the safety of our known boundaries? Is it because only then we are awakened to the possibility of visions of God and to the sound of his voice?

Chapter 1 of Ezekiel records an incredible vision of the glory of God. It is like reading a science fiction novel about extra-terrestrial beings with wings beating like the roar of rushing waters, creature faces strangely configured, metallic surfaces gleaming and steaming, wind and light playing off against one another—and rising above it all, a figure like that of a human being.

'This was the appearance of the likeness of the glory of the Lord. When I saw it, I fell face down, and I heard the voice of one speaking' (1:28).

The glory of the Lord. That is an idea, a concept or a reality that slips through my thoughts as soon as it leaves its fragrance in my mind. I sort of know what it means and then immediately I don't. A vision of glory helps me hold this elusive reality for a few seconds—but then, maybe the glory of the Lord is not holdable. Perhaps it is not meant to be clung to but rather responded to. Falling face down seems an appropriate response.

God certainly expected Ezekiel to respond to this vision! In fact, the Spirit of God raised Ezekiel to his feet so that he could listen to the voice speaking to him—because the message of God's voice is as important as the vision of God's glory. And what is the message? God in his glory is calling his people back to himself.

God of glory, awaken us to the wonder of your glory. Call us back to
yourself.

EP

Mourning and woes

I saw a hand stretched out to me. In it was a scroll, which he unrolled before me. On both sides of it were written words of lament and mourning and woe.

I can barely manage to watch a complete news broadcast on TV any more—there is so much gloom and doom and destruction. So much violence and hatred on both a global and an individual scale. I get quite depressed with what is happening in our world. Wars and bombings, abuse and misuse, lies and justification for lies —it wearies me.

Has the world always been like this or am I simply losing perspective? The world seemed safer when I was a kid; or maybe I understood my childhood world more than I understand my adult world?

Reading the book of Ezekiel clarifies my perspective. The world has always been the way it is now: chaotic, crazy, cruel. Ezekiel wrote during a time of great political upheaval, power struggles and intrigue—somewhat like our world today.

Ours is a world that puts fear into our hearts, mistrust into our relationships and deceitfulness into our agreements. A world where lament and mourning and woe are enmeshed with manipulation and corruption and lies. This is our world.

God called Ezekiel to speak his message of judgment into the chaotic, crazy world situation: 'Go to my people—a rebellious, obstinate and stubborn people and speak my words to this nation… speak my words to them, whether they listen or fail to listen… do not be afraid of what they say or terrified by them… though briers and thorns are all around you and you live among scorpions… listen to what I say to you' (2:3–8).

God is sending us a warning to sit up and take notice of what he is saying. Our life and our world depend on it.

God of this world, give us courage to lament and mourn the woes of our world. Open our eyes to see both ourselves and our world clearly, and ears to hear what you are saying to both.

EP

A passionate response

*The Spirit then lifted me up and took me away, and I went in
bitterness and in the anger of my spirit, with the strong hand of the
Lord upon me... I sat among them for seven days—overwhelmed.*

I was angry. I felt the intensity of anger welling up within me. What
other response was reasonable when this woman talked of intentional, ceremonial, ritual abuse. She was a child when all this
happened—but a child capable of knowing and remembering that
something evil was happening. Evil perpetrated by her mother, a
person she should have been able to trust—who should have been
protecting her.

I was overwhelmed as I was enveloped by her story.

Ezekiel's vision had swept him into the very presence of the love
and the holiness of the Sovereign God. He found himself caught up
in feeling the sting of rejection as God's people chose lesser gods to
love. He felt humiliation as God's love and protection was tossed
aside for more fickle titillation and useless alliances.

In listening to God's story, Ezekiel identified with God's holy and
righteous anger, knowing that his people trifled with the love of
God. With the one who had formed them into a people. So he sat
among the exiles—overwhelmed. Overwhelmed at their foolishness
and their blindness. Overwhelmed because he was called to speak
into their rejection and self-centeredness.

In so doing, Ezekiel draws us into a fresh awareness that God's
love and his concern for his people are both the prerequisite and the
source of his anger. If God did not love us, he would not feel such
passionate anger at those things that sever that bond of love.

Such anger is never comfortable—it is not meant to be, but it is
a holy and a passionate response of the profound love of an everlasting God.

---

*Everlasting God, let us taste your love and do not prevent us from
experiencing your anger when our relationship with you is broken by
our foolishness.*

EP

Lies of leadership

... they lead my people astray, saying, 'Peace', when there is no
peace, and because, when a flimsy wall is built,
they cover it with whitewash.

The Spirit of God was present in a very powerful way convicting
many of us of sin. It was one of those moments that was both awful
and sweet, saturated in both the shock of conviction and the mercy
of God.

We were in a small group at a conference. One woman burst into
sobs pouring out her confession of the sin in her life. Her sobs welled
up from the very core of her being. Almost immediately, another
well-meaning person tried to console her by short-circuiting the
God-ordained journey of conviction, repentance and confession:
'That's OK, dear. That's just human nature—don't feel bad.'

There was a collective sucking in of breath as we felt the too-
quick-to-feel-good response dousing the power of the Holy Spirit to
cleanse, purify and set this woman free of her sin. Feeling bad is
exactly the right response to conviction by the Spirit.

'Peace, peace' when there is no peace. 'Peace, peace' when we
build flimsy walls of understanding and whitewash how much God
hates sin—not because he is vindictive but because he hates the
barriers and obstacles that break and violate genuine relationship
with him. In our own discomfort with the conviction that comes
with the presence and the power of the Holy Spirit, we have a ten-
dency to dilute God's healing work in us and in his people. We get
out our bucket of paint and whitewash sin that is destroying the very
core of our lives. How much better to bring sin to God—confess it,
nail it to the cross and leave it there.

Jesus says that the truth will set us free—not a bucket of whitewash and feel-good-theology. Our hope is in truth; our freedom is in
truth—even when it hurts like hell. Maybe hell is clinging to the
whitewashed wall we put up.

God of truth, expose our whitewashed lies and release us into the free-
dom of truth.

EP

Bad shepherds

Woe to the shepherds of Israel who only take care of themselves!

As I arrived at the church to spend three days facilitating a recon-
ciliation process in a church that was divided, I walked past the
rectory where the pastor and his young student girlfriend were
washing dishes in the kitchen. The pastor's wife and his three
teenage children had already moved out, while he stayed on as the
pastor. The church had taken sides in this issue and was now
divided.

It was another story of a shepherd getting lost. It was another
'another': another pastor divorced; another clergy family devastated; like others I have come across—another book written by a
church leader claiming that Mary wasn't a virgin; another claim that
Jesus was gay; another political power play for position and status by
our pastoral leaders; another sermon where Jesus is not mentioned;
another sleek evangelist lining his already fat pockets...

God had a very clear message through Ezekiel for his clergy: 'Woe
to the shepherds of Israel who only take care of themselves' (v. 2).
'You have not strengthened the weak or healed the sick or bound up
the injured. You have not brought back the strays or searched for
the lost' (v. 4). 'Is it not enough for you to feed on the good pasture?
Must you also trample the rest of your pasture with your feet? Must
you also muddy the [water] with your feet?' (v. 18)

Thank God that the Good Shepherd responds: 'I myself will tend
my sheep and have them lie down... I will search for the lost and
bring back the strays. I will bind up the injured and strengthen the
weak, but the sleek and the strong I will destroy' (v. 15).

---

*Good Shepherd, guard the weak sheep from being bullied, lead thirsty
sheep to clear water, provide safe pasture for your sheep who have
been wounded and frightened by bad shepherds. Shield your lambs.
Shepherd us, Good Shepherd.*

Take time to pray for your church leaders today.

EP

Bad sheep

My people come to you, as they usually do, and sit before you to
listen to your words, but they do not put them into practice.
With their mouths they express devotion, but their hearts
are greedy for unjust gain.

In chapter 33, we read what God says about the people that Ezekiel
was sent to speak to. It is not a very flattering description of God's
people. What had happened to the people of God, that they have
ended up like this?

Last November I realized that I was in trouble. I am a missionary,
but my heart had grown hard and cold. I asked myself the question,
How did I get here? I never meant to wander so far away—I had
simply strayed off into bitterness, resentment and mistrust; I had,
over time, lost my way, forgetting to keep my eyes on the Good
Shepherd.

Circumstances and events had nibbled into my life, wounding
me. That in turn had opened doors for coldness and hardness to
come in and make themselves at home in my heart. And I had let
them set up house.

My good missionary words said one thing, but my heart said
another. I was like those whom Ezekiel was addressing: resistant to
the voice of God that called me to forgive and be free. Did I think
God's judgment and conviction would miss me? 'Surely the land has
been given to us as our possession' (v. 24). Why do we need to fear
that judgment will fall on us?

But judgment does fall on God's people, and God's conviction
did fall on me. God's people were taken captive into a foreign land
and they lost possession of their own pasture.

God of conviction and salvation, create in us a pure heart, a steadfast
spirit within, a willing spirit to sustain us. Do not take your Holy
Spirit from us. Restore to us the joy of your salvation (Psalm 51).

                                                                    EP

God departs

*Then the glory of the Lord departed from over
the threshold of the temple.*

It was a very impressive building, with beautiful carved wooden rail-
ings and altar. 'The largest Anglophone church in Montreal in
1955,' the wizened warden said—one of the 18 members left in this
church. 'In the good old days we had a Sunday school of 450 and
regularly had 500 in church every Sunday.'

So what happened that there were only 18 members left now?
Well, slowly the church died: their hearts had turned to other gods;
their pride changed their worship into ritual; their minds reasoned
them into an agnostic faith; and church and the God of their church
were no longer convenient or necessary. God was not even wanted
any more.

Then the Spirit of God departed.

God tells Ezekiel, their sin 'is exceedingly great; the land is full of
bloodshed and the city is full of injustice'. The people respond: 'The
Lord has forsaken the land; the Lord does not see' (9:9). 'They are
doing things that drive me far from my sanctuary,' he says (8:6).

Does God not care, does he not see when his people turn away
from him? Oh, yes, he cares and he sees, but he will not violate the
freedom of choice that he has given us when we deliberately choose
to sin and shut him out, when we 'have eyes to see but do not see
and ears to hear but do not hear, for [we] are a rebellious people'
(12:2).

There comes a point at which the Spirit of God will not, maybe
cannot, tolerate sin and the rejection of his people, and so, God
withdraws his favour and his glory departs (10:18). In sadness, he is
forced into a 'tough love' approach, in hope that once again his
people will listen and turn back to him with love.

---

*Pray for your church today and for the other churches in your area:
God of glory, return again to dwell with us in our churches and in
our hearts.*

EP

How then can we live?

*Our offences and sins weigh us down, and we are wasting away
because of them. How then can we live?*

How can we live when the glory of the Lord departs? How do we
survive the absence of God's presence?

It was a terrifying, suffocating feeling. I realized at that moment
that there was nothing I could do to restore my salvation—I could
only throw myself on the mercy of God. I was the one who had left
the relationship. I was the one who had found the drama of the ministry more important than my relationship of love and worship of
God himself.

It hadn't seemed like an out-and-out rebellion, but more an ero-
sion of focus. My ministry continued to be successful but inside my
heart was hardening. I was slowly dying—and I didn't realize it until
my spirit was dead. How naive could I be! Thinking that ministry—
the doing stuff of my faith—was the real thing. What God really
wanted was my heart and my love, not me doing stuff.

Then the unspeakable, the unthinkable happened: God's presence departed—his glory had gone (10:18). I was the one who had
grieved and wounded the Holy Spirit until he had no choice but to
leave.

Israel finally acknowledged their responsibility for the mess they
were in: 'Our offences and sins weigh us down, and we are wasting
away because of them. How then can we live?'

In short, without God, they could not. Israel had rejected God to
worship foreign gods. Injustice and corruption were the norm;
immorality was pervasive. Their offences and sins weighed them
down and they wasted away. Are we any different today? I think not.

---

*God of life, forgive us our offences and our sins. Release us from the
weight of our offences. Breathe new life into us today.*

*Thank God for his forgiveness to all who repent and turn to live God's
way (v. 11).*

EP

God's invitation

*As surely as I live, declares the Sovereign Lord, I take no
pleasure in the death of the wicked, but rather that they turn
from their ways and live. Turn! Turn from your evil ways!
Why will you die, O house of Israel?*

I was sitting in a meeting with young women and men in a small city
in the former Soviet Union listening as they told their stories of
when they became followers of Jesus. Instead of using the words
'becoming a Christian' many would say 'I repented on 15 January
2003' or 'I repented at summer camp last year.' It jarred me because
I so seldom hear that word 'repent' in my North American context.

I talked to some of them about that use of language. They
explained to me that people of the Soviet Union understand themselves to be Christians already because of their rich Orthodox
Christian heritage. They understood that for them to become disciples of Jesus they needed to repent of sin and receive the salvation
Jesus offers through his death on the cross.

They had such a clear understanding that repentance was essential in becoming—and being—a Christian. In fact, the Western
Church might benefit greatly from such clarity. The New Testament
word for repentance means an about turn—a 180-degree turn—to
head in a new direction. Here in the West, we don't talk about
repentance because we don't talk about sin any more. How can we
possibly repent of our sins if we don't even talk about sin? How,
then, can we turn from our evil ways and live? Those young Soviet
Christians clearly understood that; I hadn't.

Neither had the nation of Israel. God was asking them—
directly—to turn from their sin and live! He was pleading with the
Israelites to make an about face and head in a new direction that
would lead them to life.

He is inviting us to do the same.

---

*God of mercy, open our eyes to see our sin and give us courage to turn
from our sin and choose you.*

EP

Watchmen needed

I looked for a man among them who would build up the wall and stand before me in the gap on behalf of the land so I would not have to destroy it, but I found none.

How would the people of Israel turn from their wicked ways unless someone interceded for them and challenged them to change their ways? To listen to the words of God that would save them?

How will people in our own cities and towns and churches hear the truth if we do not speak it?

Many years ago, God asked me to tell my neighbours about him, but, you see, my neighbours were my friends. Their kids played with my kids. We had coffee together almost every day while our kids played together. I didn't want to lose their friendship—I mean, I had to live beside them, didn't I? I didn't want them to think I was some kind of religious freak—I might just turn them off Jesus instead of turning them on.

God continued to challenge and invite me to love them more. So, I began to pray and intercede for my neighbours, and I began to tell them about my other friend, Jesus.

It was amazing! They actually wanted to talk about my faith and the Bible. We had wonderful conversations—they actually liked my God, and they didn't think I was a freak! Today, many years later, they continue to grow in grace as godly women drawing their family members into faith alongside themselves.

Today, as in Ezekiel's day, God is looking for 'watchmen'—men and women—to stand in the gap and speak of him in our world, in our professions, in our communities, in our families—to intercede on behalf of the land so that they may turn and be saved.

Pray for the people you meet regularly: God of the watchmen, give us a vision and the courage to stand in the gap for the people in our lives.
EP

A new era

For every living soul belongs to me... I will judge you, each one according to his ways, declares the Sovereign Lord. Repent! Turn away from all your offences; then sin will not be your downfall.

Unlike most of the kids I went to school with, I really needed a job in the summer to make money to live on during the school year and to continue my education. Every January I would begin looking for a summer job. I dreaded filling out four-page applications never to hear back, but I diligently filled them out, hoping and praying that this summer I would get a good job. I had some lousy jobs, including working as a glazier in an aluminium window factory, being literally chased around my worktable every morning by an overweight foreman who was itching to get his hands on me.

My summer job experience wasn't everyone's. I had two friends who got the most amazing summer jobs in fashion stores or as airline flight attendants. I was glad for them. Who wants to glaze aluminium windows? But we all knew that they got those jobs because their father knew other fathers who pulled strings, used connections and who were part of the 'old boys' network'. They got their jobs because of connections and influence, not because of what they filled out on their application form.

In Ezekiel, God changes the ground rules of connection with him. The 'old boys' network' is gone. No longer can status or position or ethnic group or wealth open the back door into relationship with God—only personal repentance and godliness can.

A new era has come. A new nation is born. God loves each person individually and each individual stands before God on their own merit, judged by their own actions. In this new nation of God, we come as individuals who are choosing God and choosing to be formed into a people of God.

God of justice, thank you for the freedom and the dignity of being able to come to you based simply on who we are before you.

EP

A new hope

I will give you a new heart and put a new spirit in you; I will remove from you your heart of stone and give you a heart of flesh. And I will put my Spirit in you and move you to follow my decrees and be careful to keep my laws.

This new era of justice, of being responded to individually, brings new hope to each individual: the hope of a new heart and a new spirit. Thank God, it's not up to us to do it—God will do it!

Listen to the language: 'I will give you a new heart and put a new spirit in you; I will remove from you your heart of stone and give you a heart of flesh. And I will put my Spirit in you...' says the Lord.

Most of my life I have struggled and strained to do it right! Thinking that if I do it right, I will be acceptable and loved. It has taken me years to lay this down at Jesus' feet, admitting that I cannot do it right. If I could do it right, I wouldn't need Jesus to save me and I wouldn't need the Spirit to empower me—I actually wouldn't need God at all! I wouldn't need anyone else either.

For years this drive towards perfectionism, a drive rooted in fear and shame of who I really am, has robbed me of peace, gentleness, self-respect and dignity. Gently and tenderly, Jesus beckons me to lean into him, to rest in him—a totally foreign concept to me. Slowly he is forming a kinder, gentler, softer heart of flesh in me and giving me a new spirit that can soar on the wind no matter how strong or gentle it blows.

God of hope, put your Spirit in us. Change our heart of stone into a heart of flesh. Teach us to lean into you and to lay down our need to live life perfectly by ourselves and in our own strength.

EP

New life from old bones

*'Son of man, can these bones live?' I said, 'O Sovereign Lord,
you alone know.'*

In Ezekiel chapter 37 there is a wonderful vision of dry bones
rattling into life so vividly written that I will let it speak for itself. In
the vision, the Spirit of the Lord sets Ezekiel down in a valley full of
dry bones. As Ezekiel prophesizes, the bones begin to rattle and
move. Tendons and flesh appear; skin and muscle appear; but there
is no breath in them.

Then God, himself, addresses the dry bones: 'I will make breath
enter you, and you will come to life. I will attach tendons to you and
make flesh come upon you and cover you with skin; I will put breath
in you, and you will come to life. Then you will know that I am the
Lord.'

'Come from the four winds, O breath, and breathe into these
slain, that they may live' and breath entered them; they came to life
and stood up on their feet—a vast army.

Ezekiel goes back to the people and tells of this vision and finally
the people get it! They cry out: 'Our bones are dried up and our
hope is gone; we are cut off.'

God replies: 'O my people, I am going to open your graves and
bring you up from them... then you, my people, will know that I am
the Lord... I will put my Spirit in you and you will live, and I will
settle you in your own land. Then you will know that I the Lord
have spoken, and I have done it, declares the Lord.'

When people turn back to God, God, in turn, makes a promise:
I will give you my Spirit and I will take you home.

---

*God of breath, breathe into our dry bones in our land that we may
know that you are the Lord and that it is you—you alone—that gives
breath and life to our dry bones and dead flesh.*

EP

A new presence—God is back!

My dwelling-place will be with them; I will be their God, and they will be my people. Then the nations will know that I the Lord make Israel holy, when my sanctuary is among them for ever.

We walked down the most derelict, dismal student dormitory hallway I have ever been in. We were in Sevastopol in Crimea. We could see the shadows of students in the hallway. We were unable to see their faces in the faint light from the single 40-watt bulb for a 150-foot length of hallway. Two dogs were scurrying around looking for food. There were holes in the crumbling cement of the floor, the walls were peeling—an ancient paint job of institutional green, the toilets were dirty and in serious disrepair. It was overwhelmingly dark.

Then we entered one of the dormitory rooms to join a Christian student group. I wasn't prepared for what we experienced: the presence of God was palpable in this room.

There were about a dozen students meeting to worship and study the Bible. We sat on tattered, rickety spring beds and a few squeaky, wobbly chairs. As we sang praises in Russian and Ukrainian, the students' faces began to glow with the glory of God. A warm presence filled the room with a sweet fragrance of joy and gratitude. It was overwhelmingly light.

God was dwelling with them in that place—his glory was upon and within them. God was there.

That is the promise of God for his people: to dwell with them wherever they are. That is his desire. Not just with a select few but for all nations and all people. He will make his name known among the people and the nations will know that he is the Lord, the Holy One (39:7).

Where God dwells, there is healing and life (chapter 47), and where he dwells, he will pour out his Spirit on his people (39:29).

God of healing and life, dwell among us and make us holy. Pour out your Spirit upon us.

EP

Prayer first

Very early in the morning, while it was still dark, Jesus got up,
left the house and went off to a solitary place, where he prayed.

Mark's Gospel boldly asks us to respond to Jesus the man, and
vividly reveals the humanity and compassion of Jesus the servant.
This colourful Gospel account includes scenes of family life,
glimpses of human-interest stories, and the often-comical fallibility
of the disciples. It is easy to believe that these words were based on
the first hand and very personal account of Peter, with whom Mark
travelled.

In the opening chapter, we see Jesus spending an evening at
Peter's house, where he healed not only Peter's mother-in-law, but
also the 'many' who came to him for healing and deliverance.

Jesus is not in the business of demonstrating his power through
these early miracles; indeed he forbids the demons he cast out from
naming him. Rather he is concerned with meeting needs. He liber-
ates those who come to him from sickness and evil, so that they can
live life to the full, as God intended. Teaching the good news of the
kingdom is central to Jesus' mission.

Leading Methodist, the late Donald English wrote, 'Everything
that is done or said in the service of God must be in harmony with
the good news of the kingdom.' 'That is why I have come,' says
Jesus, and he promptly takes his bewildered disciples off on a
preaching tour, but he only embarked on that tour once he had
rested and spent time with his Father in prayer and communion. If
Jesus needed to do that before beginning his work, how much more
do we?

As we begin our own tour of Mark's Gospel, and reflect on the
servanthood and compassion of Jesus the Son, let us first spend time
with God the Father.

Father God, may we follow your itinerary as we take this reflective
tour of the life of your Son. Show us not only the humanity of Jesus,
but also our need to respond.

WB

Filled with compassion

A man with leprosy came to him and begged him on his knees,
'If you are willing, you can make me clean.' Filled with
compassion, Jesus reached out his hand and touched the man.
'I am willing,' he said. 'Be clean!'

Jesus was never afraid to shock. It was love that motivated his actions, not a desire to do the acceptable thing, please all the people all the time or run a good PR campaign.

Faced with a man crippled and disfigured by leprosy he reached out with compassion, love and not a little anger at the way this man's life and body were so marred. Leprosy made this man an 'untouchable'. He was isolated in an underworld, an outcast. He was the last on the list of the lost. The first in the queue for the scrapheap of life.

We can almost hear the gasps of bystanders as Jesus' fingers touch scarred skin of a man who must have forgotten what it was like to be touched by another human being. That touch in itself must have brought healing, which was as much emotional as physical.

Jesus so naturally and lovingly crosses social and religious boundaries of acceptability. Such actions are fundamental to his being. With love as his motivation, he meets the need and offers love without regard for the consequences. How attractive that boldness must have been. How overwhelming for those he looked upon with tenderness and released into wholeness. Sadly, the miracle, not the man, drew the attention and misunderstanding of bystanders, and the love at the heart of it was missed.

We so often look at the outside rather than at the heart. Jesus challenges us to be unshockable and unafraid to shock when we are motivated by love. To cross boundaries and defy convention when the needy and the unlovable need his touch. Are we willing?

Lead me to those who need your touch, Lord. Make my love unshockable. Remind me whose hand I am stretching out and whose love I am sharing.

WB

Through the roof

Some men came, bringing to him a paralytic, carried by four of them. Since they could not get him to Jesus because of the crowd, they made an opening in the roof above Jesus and... lowered the mat the paralysed man was lying on.

Without being mean to the men, isn't this just the kind of thing us girls would do? Aren't we the ones who plan a 'trip of a lifetime' for a terminally ill friend or trundle her wheelchair breathlessly up a hill so that she can see 'that view' one more time?

Here are at least four friends, some carrying, some along for the fun, chipping through the roof to meet Jesus. It is such a vivid scene to imagine, isn't it? Upturned faces fixed on the ceiling, while dust and debris flutter down with the invading sunlight. No wonder Jesus offered healing and forgiveness 'when he saw their faith', but he must have been amused by it all too! Once again, he simply restores a life to wholeness. We cannot fail to be inspired by the dogged determination and faith of these friends. I would love to have heard their conversation as they did their gospel equivalent of trundling the wheelchair up the hill.

'But what if we can't get in?' asks a wavering one. 'We'll just go through the roof!' says the boldest. Allowing the hilarity of this suggestion to spur them on, their faith literally gets them through!

I wish my faith were the roof-smashing kind! But I doubt that they would have made their appearance without the encouragement, fun and faith they shared together. They depended on each other, not just to get through the roof, but to believe they could do it in the first place. When they dared to go with their faith-filled plan, they met Jesus who recognized and rewarded it.

I think they met the warmth of his amused smile, too.

Lord, make my faith the 'roof-smashing' kind and let me recognize the warmth of your smile.

WB

49

Bad company

While Jesus was having dinner at Levi's house, many tax collectors and 'sinners' were eating with him and his disciples, for there were many who followed him.

Once again, Jesus crosses cultural barriers of acceptability in order to meet those who need him most. Levi showed no hesitation in following Jesus, according to Mark's account. This could be Mark's sharp writing style, but it is just as likely to be Levi's sharp business practice. Here was a man used to making tough decisions and closing lightning deals in order to get what he wanted.

Levi was not afraid of rising to a challenge. The challenge to follow Jesus was compelling. Levi had more than a few reasons to ask, 'Why me?' Tax collectors were not only guilty of extortion, often of the poor, but their meeting with ritually unclean gentile traders was frowned upon. Levi really was bad company. To eat with him as Jesus did, was risky in the extreme, but Jesus, as ever, puts love first. Sometimes we have to make tough decisions about how much we share the lives of others if we are to bring them the love of Jesus through genuine friendship.

If we always avoid difficult people and situations for fear of 'slipping up', feeling uneasy out of our comfort zone or being seen with the wrong crowd in the wrong places, we will inadvertently keep Jesus away from those who need him most.

We shouldn't put ourselves at unconsidered risk, but neither should we wrap ourselves up in Christian subcultural cotton wool to such an extent that it fills our ears and deafens us to what has effectively become an outside world.

Jesus spent time with those who needed him most. If we can be bold enough to do the same, our faith and witness will be empowered and we will know more of what answering Jesus' call to 'Follow me' really means.

Saviour, as I follow you, lead me into the lives of those who need you most, so that they can choose to follow you too.

WB

Meeting needs

When Jesus landed and saw a large crowd, he had compassion on them, because they were like sheep without a shepherd. So he began teaching them many things.

The disciples' mood has dropped after the euphoria of a hectic day. Tired and hungry, they want Jesus to send this needy crowd away to find food, but Jesus, inwardly moved, is unable to do so, and suggests that the disciples feed them.

Imagine their incredulity! 'Haven't we done enough already?' Preaching, teaching, crowd control, and now they are asked to become celebrity chefs! They protest that this is hardly the spot for an out-of-town supermarket and that, even if it were, their pay wouldn't stretch that far.

Jesus patiently directs them to what they already have and asks them to work with that. Yes, it was a miracle, but it wasn't planned as such. This was simply Jesus' love in action—the result of compassion in the face of need that left him inwardly moved enough to have to do something about it. The result was God's abundant provision.

When our inward response to the needs of others moves us enough to make us want to 'do something about it', it is likely to be a genuine response to the Holy Spirit's prompting: 'You give them something.' However overwhelming the need, we can always simply begin with what we have. God will do the rest.

Last summer a youth drama group from our church went to train and entertain other young people through an outreach project in Bulgaria. They had already put on excellent productions 'at home' but their leaders, Richard and Teena, have a passion for mission that meets needs.

Their 'don't just sit there, do something' approach was infectious and caught the imagination of their young team. By taking their drama to Bulgaria, they used what they had in terms of gifts and resources to meet the needs that had so moved them.

They responded to Jesus' request: 'You give them something.'

Lord, are you telling me, 'You give them something'?

WB

Children welcome

Whoever welcomes one of these little children in my name
welcomes me; and whoever welcomes me does not welcome me
but the one who sent me.

The disciples have been at it again, allowing themselves to become
puffed up by their role in Jesus' ministry, even arguing about which
one of them is the greatest. They make a comical bunch with their
jostling for position and self-proclaimed pecking order, but their
motivation and misunderstanding needs serious response.

Jesus, in his wisdom, takes this as his cue for a series of teaching
sessions for the disciples, using the little children he so obviously
loved spending time with as an illustration. The disciples badly
needed to understand that the way of Jesus does not involve con-
ventional 'greatness' but servanthood. Not jostling to be first, but
joyfully putting yourself last. Not being the greatest but the least; as
a little child.

Children held a lowly place in the Greco-Roman world. That
Jesus should spend time with children, let alone bring them before
the disciples as a positive example would have been very difficult for
them to swallow. It takes more than one lesson before the disciples
recognize the powerful message of the little child before them.

They would gradually understand that, in welcoming the lowliest,
they were welcoming not just Jesus but also the God of the universe.
If that was not a big enough thought, they also had to grasp that not
only is the kingdom for children, too, it needs to be welcomed as
children would welcome it. In short, the Big Guys have a lot to learn
from the Little Ones.

There is a direct challenge here to all of us regarding our children's ministry. Do we regard our Sunday school and junior church
as little more than a baby-sitting service for the 'real worship' that
is adult church? Are children and young people just too noisy/
demanding/unpredictable for us? How often do we expect to learn
something of God through our little ones?

Father, make me like a little child.

WB

Wide-eyed

I tell you the truth, anyone who will not receive the kingdom of God like a little child will never enter it.

Here is Jesus' second teaching session on the example and value of children. Still slow to learn, the disciples are actively discouraging parents from bringing their children to Jesus. They couldn't understand how much Jesus loved them! Don't exclude them, he says, be like them, learn from them.

Jesus explains that he wants children included because they are a perfect example of how to joyfully enter God's kingdom. As a child is dependent on his parent in every area of his life, in total trust, so it should be with our heavenly Father. These little ones have no hidden agenda, no personal ambition or ulterior motive, just a desire to be with Jesus and to be blessed by him. As they run to him, Jesus lifts them onto his lap, takes them in his arms and blesses them.

With each child, the disciples are provided with a warm, living (and probably giggling) illustration of the kind of faith God requires. A faith that is wide-eyed with wonder. Trusting and accepting. A faith that sends us running into the arms of Jesus at his bidding, and that tilts our chin to look up into the eyes of God. It is an illustration we see around us so often in our own families, among the children of friends, in the games of parents in the park. It is the simplest most profound illustration of the kind of relationship God longs to have with us. He could not make it more obvious, but, so often, just like the disciples, we dismiss the childlike because we cannot believe it is what is wanted. We cannot believe it can be that simple, but Jesus says it is. We are to come to him as little children.

Father, you have made me like a little child. Teach me to run to you with my arms outstretched. Lift me in your arms, and hold me close and wide-eyed, 'For such is the kingdom.'

WB

Give it up

*Jesus looked at him and loved him. 'One thing you lack,' he said.
'Go, sell everything you have and give to the poor, and you will
have treasure in heaven. Then come, follow me.'*

As Jesus leaves the hubbub of children, a wealthy young man runs
to him and falls on his knees at Jesus' feet. He is, as we would now
call it, 'searching'. He lives a religious life but wants more. Something, or someone, is missing.

That 'someone' now stands before him, with a tender heart:
'Jesus looked at him and loved him', recognizing in this young man,
an earnest and genuine search for the truth: 'What must I do?'

Jesus answers that he must give up his wealth, for it leaves him
'lacking'. He is not implying that the rich cannot enter the kingdom
of God, rather that they will have to change their basis of security
from trust in money to trust in him. For many, like this young man,
that change is too difficult to contemplate. Jesus loved this young
man, yet he did not argue, force him to follow or admonish him for
his choice. The choice was his, and he could still choose the one
who loves him.

Recently I took a close friend along to a *Christianity Explored*
course. She joined the course happily, with a genuine desire to find
God. As I had been praying for her for 16 years, my desire was just
as strong! She chatted in discussions, listened thoughtfully to the
talks and shared long heart-to-hearts on the journey home, but at
the end of the course, unlike many others, she did not decide to
follow Jesus. She wishes she could share my faith, but cannot, yet,
make the choice. I cannot help but feel sad, but I will keep praying.
She could still choose to go his way, because Jesus looks at her and
loves her.

'*For where your treasure is, there your heart will be also*' (Matthew
6:21). May all my riches be in you, Lord.

WB

Servant of all

*For even the Son of Man did not come to be served, but to serve,
and to give his life as a ransom for many.*

Here is another reminder for the disciples about the nature of true
greatness. They had been squabbling among themselves, and missing the point, as usual. Jesus turns the values of their world upside
down by insisting that to be first is to be a slave. We can almost see
the brain cogs turning as the disciples attempt to work that one out!
It's all gibberish to them because they still don't speak the kingdom
language.

They are holding on to a worldview which does not understand
that in God's kingdom, greatness is characterized by how much we
serve others, not by how much we are served. Jesus offered himself
as a supreme example of servanthood, prepared to give everything,
including himself, to those he had come to serve and save. We are
not told what the disciples' reaction was to Jesus' words. Perhaps
they were so busy chewing over the implications of having to be
slaves to one another that they missed his final words!

When we think of Christian service we often come up with an
image of a begrudging, duty-bound kind of Christianity. Yet, serving
one another can be pure joy, an act of worship and, very often, fun!

A few weeks ago, our 13-year-old son gave up his Sunday lie-in
to help us accompany patients at our local hospital from their wards
to the chapel for a Sunday service. He wheeled wheelchairs and
beds alongside the adults, puffing a little as he did it, but silently
pushing and grinning his way around the hospital.

Afterwards he shared how much he had enjoyed the experience,
and said, 'I'm glad I went. It gave me something special I can't
explain.' He had discovered the joy of servanthood.

Lord, make me servant of all.

*These verses echo the haunting anthem of the suffering servant in
Isaiah 53. You might like to read it to remind yourself of its theme.*
                                     WB

'Rabbi, I want to see!'

'What do you want me to do for you?' Jesus asked him.
The blind man said, 'Rabbi, I want to see!' 'Go,' said Jesus,
'your faith has healed you.' Immediately he received his sight
and followed Jesus along the road.

Here is a man who knows what he wants. He wants Jesus! In contrast to the tired and dawdling disciples dragging behind in the
crowd, Bartimaeus runs forward to Jesus at the first signal. Despite
the fact that he cannot see, he knows exactly where he is going!

It is his faith in the Jesus he recognizes, even in his blindness,
that frames this drama of regained sight. It is as if his faith is the
most important thing, his restored sight an afterthought. Why else
would Jesus ask a blind man what he wants?

Bartimaeus wants to see physically, but the real joy is that he
already has his spiritual sight. In that astonishing faith he is immediately healed, and follows Jesus along the road, with more than a
little enthusiasm! I have a hunch that his enthusiasm might have
proved just a tiny bit tiresome to the weary disciples.

When those of us who have been Christians for some time meet
those who have recently recognized Jesus, like Bartimaeus, we can
often share the disciples' attitude. Oh, we are overjoyed that they
have become Christians, too, but we can be almost amused at what
we think is a naive first flush of faith.

'They'll get over it,' we think. 'They'll soon settle down.' We are
like the disciples, dragging our feet along in the dust and failing to
recognize the unique joy of those who rejoice in their newfound
sight. Perhaps we should offer to walk with them a while as they
follow Jesus along the road. Knock the dust off our feet and enjoy
the refreshment of their fellowship. We need to open our eyes to
recognize that this is Jesus we are following! Don't we want to see
him too?

Open my eyes to you afresh, Lord.

WB

Something out of nothing

They all gave out of their wealth; but she, out of her poverty, put in everything—all she had to live on.

From where Jesus was sitting in the temple he could watch what people were putting into the offering. (No neat wooden boxes with note-thin slits here then!) It may seem an odd thing for Jesus to do, but he wasn't interested in the wealth carried in people's hands, rather the wealth carried in their hearts.

The rich gave with a show of ostentatious generosity, glancing left and right to see who would notice them give. Some had hidden agendas bound away in their gifts, deals with men, even deals with God.

Probably no one but Jesus watched the widow drop her two small copper coins alongside the bulging moneybags. If they did, it would probably have been with unseeing eyes or even contempt, but Jesus watched her, with love and compassion. Her gift was so important that he called his disciples to him to tell them so. Jesus knew that this widow had not only given from her poverty of income, but also from her generosity of faith. She had given all she had to give.

Jesus still watches what we give, but his issue isn't a financial one. He looks to see whether we hold him at the centre of our giving; whether we give all we have to give in terms of gifts, time, energy and love, as well as money; and whether we give in total trust in his provision and commitment to his purposes.

Jesus doesn't want the leftovers of our lives. The spare moments and the days off. He wants to share the first thoughts of the day, hold our seven-day week, enjoy the best of our God-given gifts. He wants us to give it all—give and give until our hands are empty—but only because he has so much to give back that we will need our empty hands to begin to receive it all.

Jesus, you can have it all.

WB

Extravagant love

*'Leave her alone,' said Jesus. 'Why are you bothering her? She
has done a beautiful thing to me.'*

I so wish I had been this woman! She knew just how to give extrav-
agant love to her Lord! After pouring expensive oil on his head, she
broke the jar, signifying that all the oil was for this one special occasion. Hers is a passionate and dramatic response of gratitude. One
of those 'I wish I'd thought of it first' moments.

Could she have known the significance of what she had done?
Jesus was 'the anointed one of God', yet preparing to die. She was
encouraging him at this difficult point, not only by expressing her
love, but by anointing him for his death.

The disciples have a point. The sale of the oil would have helped
the poor. However, in saying so, they once again showed that they
missed the bigger point. They were unaware of the historical significance of the moment and the eternal significance of the man.

This is a moment that won't be forgotten, Jesus said. Because of
her love, this woman will be part of his story. She led the way of love
and devotion, which other women followed throughout the rest of
Jesus' life. It was their faithfulness and devotion that supported him,
and it is they who were able to identify most closely with his humanity, his suffering and his death.

Sometimes I know moments of ecstatic delight in the loveliness
of Jesus. Moments of immense gratitude, sheer joy and bewildering
wonder. They are few and far between, probably because I have too
many 'stuffy disciple' moments. (Am I too hard on these poor men?)

When those moments happen, I believe I feel as this woman felt.
Generous, spontaneous and searching for some way to express my
almost uncontrollable love for my Lord. I call them my 'oil-on-his-
head moments'! The really exciting thing is that Jesus loves them
just as much. He says, 'She has done a beautiful thing!'

Lord, bend your head so that I can pour the oil!

WB

The most intimate prayer

'Abba, Father,' he said, 'everything is possible for you. Take this cup from me. Yet not what I will, but what you will.'

The disciples, tired and frightened, fell asleep while Jesus prayed. Only Jesus knew what lay ahead, and Mark uses some powerful verbs to describe his anguish... 'distressed'... 'troubled'... 'overwhelmed with sorrow'.

Reading Jesus' prayer is like creeping up to his side in the darkness to listen, helplessly, to his struggle. I want to reach out and say, 'I will stay awake for you, Lord.' Don't you? But would we?

His words to his Father, Abba—Daddy—are intimate and raw. He is hanging on by a thread to his Father's love: 'Is there any way out, Father? Must I go through this?' But his Father's will is paramount. 'Not my will, but yours.'

Five years ago, I received an advanced cancer diagnosis just before Good Friday. I knelt in church, listening to those words of Jesus, and wrote later: 'Those words, read out this afternoon, echoed with meaning... although they seemed almost whispered by the reader, it was as if they bounced off the cold stone walls and hurled themselves at me. I was glad to be on my knees. I felt that if I had been standing I would have been knocked off balance. Lord, I know you are in this. What is it about? Where are you leading me? I feel in possession of a dark, fearful, unexplored yet wonderful treasure; that I might glorify your name. I can identify with those words of Jesus. Even though my suffering will be so much less, I know that mixture of feelings: of knowing you must be in the darkness with me, but also feeling abandoned' (*In the Palm of God's Hand* by Wendy Bray).

Jesus surrendered himself into the safe eternal arms of his Father. I could do nothing less.

'It would be just another illusion to believe that reaching out to God will free us from pain and suffering. Often, indeed, it will take us where we would rather not go.'
HENRI NOUWEN

WB

And so...

*Then the disciples went out and preached everywhere,
and the Lord worked with them and confirmed his word
by the signs that accompanied it.*

At the very beginning of our fortnight of readings, we learnt that
Mark set out to show us Jesus, in all his humanity, compassion and
servanthood and that he asked for a response from his readers. Now,
at the very end, we witness the response made by the men and
women living alongside Jesus.

They have been through so much together, knowing extremes of
love and loss, and now, reunion and commission. The risen Jesus
appears to his followers and tells them what they must do in
response both to the life he has lived and to the life that he offers.

They are to tell the whole world about him, assured that all who
believe will be saved, but knowing that those who do not believe
will be condemned. He promises to equip them for the work they
have to do by giving special gifts and abilities, signs and wonders, to
those who faithfully engage in mission: 'Then the disciples went out
and preached everywhere, and the Lord worked with them...'

What a turnaround in the hearts and minds of these followers of
Jesus. At last their eyes were opened and they spoke the language
of the kingdom as true citizens. At last they saw the real point, recognized who Jesus was and did what he told them, without question!
They could do nothing else in response to the man whom they had
lived with and loved for so long.

We have had two short weeks living in the Gospel of Mark with
Jesus. We have known his humanity, felt his compassion, watched
his servanthood and experienced his astonishing love. How will we
respond?

Who walks with you, yet doesn't wish to follow?
Who hears you speak, forgetting every word?
Who feels your touch and doesn't hang on tightly?
Or hears your laugh to miss it on the wind?
Not I, Lord.
I live and love, for you.

WB

God's upside-down kingdom

But many who are first will be last, and the last will be first.

This verse accompanies the parable of the labourers in the vineyard. Those who have worked a full day in the heat are shocked to find that the generous landowner pays them exactly the same as the people waiting nearly all day to be hired—all receive a full day's pay. Surely, they feel, we who worked the hardest deserve more.

We have probably all grown up with the words 'it's not fair' ringing in our ears. Jesus points out that nobody got paid less than proper, it was just that the landowner was exceptionally generous to hire the ones who would normally have gone home hungry. Things are different in God's upside-down kingdom!

At various times in our life we probably identify with both groups of workers. Sometimes we are the hard-working righteous ones, helping out at yet another church event when we would rather be at home watching television, going to the gym or having a quiet meal with friends. This parable shows us that leading blameless lives—even looking after elderly parents, screaming children and demanding spouses—doesn't make us more special than anyone else in God's eyes. Because the amazing thing is, that God has no favourites, and loves us all equally.

This is a very comforting thought when we are identifying with the labourers hired at the last minute, when everyone else seems to be coping better than we are and is more spiritual and altogether nicer. It is as if we are standing in the hot sun like the labourers, waiting for things to get better and fearing they never will, but God still loves us and wants to lavish his amazing generosity on us, just as in the parable. All Christians are equal in God's eyes: we are fellow workers abundantly loved and forgiven. Now that is a kingdom I want to belong to!

Try to think of someone who feels like they are one of 'the last' and hold them up in prayer to God.

WP

Upside-down love

*But I say to you, Love your enemies and pray for
those who persecute you.*

A short time ago a gang of youths started throwing stones at the
windows of our house, shouting abuse. This went on regularly for
about three weeks and was pretty unpleasant. I didn't feel much
love for the lads involved! How much worse it must be for someone
who is mugged or whose child is harmed.

Yet in God's kingdom we are asked to love our enemies. The
word used for love is *agape*—an act of the will, desiring someone's
highest good without bitterness, whatever has been done to us. It is
a victory over what comes naturally to us. It is not soft love, giving
in to unreasonable demands and being a walkover. It may involve
helping the other person to face up to themselves, but all without
bitterness on our part or the desire for revenge. We cannot even
begin to do this without God's help.

It is a clever instruction of Jesus' to tell us to pray for those we
dislike—it is very hard to hate someone when you are praying for
them. The difficulty is even wanting to pray. We are being challenged to do what Jesus did. On the cross, he prayed for his mur-
derers. In God's challenging kingdom, we are to follow the same
path. By doing this we become fully human, freed from the burden
of hatred and bitterness that can so weigh us down. We are to aston-
ish the world by the way we shine God's light of love and forgiveness into its gloomy places.

There is a Chinese story about an emperor who marched with his
soldiers to quash a rebellion in a distant province. His soldiers were
incensed when, instead of fighting, he shook hands with the rebel
leaders and invited them to a banquet. 'You promised us we would
get rid of our enemies,' they raged. 'But I have done just that,' he
replied, 'for now I have no enemies, only friends.'

Lord, help me to begin to want to pray for those I dislike.

WP

More important than wealth

Do not store up for yourselves treasures on earth, where moth and rust consume and where thieves break in and steal; but store up for yourselves treasures in heaven.

The things that this world thinks are important seem to boil down to power, wealth and sex. Jesus deals with power repeatedly—now it is the turn of wealth.

I have recently taken a job as a learning support assistant, and one of the things I have had to come to terms with is the low pay compared to my previous teaching salary. It's not that we particularly need the money, just that a certain status comes with a higher wage. I wasn't sure I could cope with being less important in my own eyes. Now I am delighted with the job—half the salary but twice the fun!

Despite the uncertainties of possessions, we are often caught extolling the value of wealth: 'Do you know how much a house down my road sold for last week?' for instance. In the East, beautiful clothes often were a sign of a person's status, such as Joseph's many-coloured coat, which set him above his brothers. We all know how fashions can change, and my daughter is at present experiencing first hand the destructive potential of the humble moth! Our treasure cannot be protected from burglars, from natural disasters, a fall in the property market or a plunge on the stock exchange. Wealth cannot be relied upon.

Jesus is not condemning wealth, just our reliance on it. He is pointing out the importance of getting our priorities right. The most important thing should be our relationship with God himself, then all the rest will fall into place. The world should be a place where we build our character, where our kindness, generosity and love for others grow. It should be where we really get to know God, so that we make the most of the 'heaven' that comes from belonging to God right now.

Lord may I have an opportunity today to 'store up treasure in heaven'.
WP

Take a risk

For those who want to save their life will lose it, and those who lose their life for my sake will find it.

I recently met a charming, intelligent and articulate woman who had given many years of faithful service to her church. She had steered the church through a very difficult time after the building had nearly fallen down. As a result she had been interviewed on local television.

She revealed that she had never told her work colleagues that she went to church and had carefully kept out of any discussion about religion. The morning after she had appeared on television she went into work worried sick that her colleagues would have seen the local news, found out about her church activities and would now treat her as odd or different. She was amazed when they sympathized with her and treated her church commitment as quite natural and interesting. She was close to tears as she said she wished she had been brave enough to talk openly years earlier.

We often go out of our way to protect ourselves from what we think are the parts of the Christian message that would put unsustainable demands on our ordered way of life. Far from losing our life, we hardly even get a little plaster-worthy scratch! We are so worried that we will 'get it wrong' that we talk ourselves into doing nothing at all.

God's kingdom is not about reaching a happy state of serene security, where we can relax and enjoy the rewards of a successful and well-lived life. There is a constant challenge to think 'out of the box' about what God is wanting us to do. What matters is being prepared to give him our all—looking back we may well see that he wants us to find a much better life than the one we are protecting at the moment.

Lord, show me what you want me to do, and help me to risk trying it.
WP

Becoming child-like

Truly I tell you, unless you change and become like children, you will never enter the kingdom.

Let me tell you about Gemma. Gemma is ten and she has some difficulties with her speech, her movements and her learning. She finds it hard to pronounce some words clearly, but, despite this, she will have a go at reading aloud. She tries very hard with school work and is getting better at using numbers. When she mastered the eight times table she was so thrilled, she recited it to anyone who would listen. Gemma shows all her emotions. If she is happy she beams a radiant smile, if she is worried she scowls, and if she is upset she crumples. She has no idea of how to deceive. She is enthusiastic about learning and she knows how to have fun.

Gemma remembers the things she knows are important to you. If you have shared a joy or worry with her, she will ask about it the next day. She trusts adults and expects them to be kind. She will give little presents to say thank you and remembers people's birthdays. She will talk to a visiting dignitary as if she was talking to a friend. If she is worried she will tell someone what is troubling her, and if something good has happened she cannot keep it to herself. Although she probably couldn't tell you much about theology, she knows that God loves her. She adores her family and is proud of what they do. She will never run her own business, be a model or go to university, but Gemma will be loved because of her innocence and kindness.

We probably all know a Gemma somewhere. When we look at ourselves in comparison, perhaps we see that we have lost something on our way to adulthood. Jesus didn't say in what way we were to become like children again, but maybe in looking at Gemma we can see what needs to be done.

Thank God for any children who are special to you and pray for their well-being.

                                                                    WP

Service

*... whoever wishes to be great among you must be your servant,
and whoever wishes to be first among you must be your slave...*

Parents could be forgiven for thinking this is one instruction that they are obeying already! 'Can you pick me up at midnight from the station, wash my sports kit for tomorrow, cook for the ten friends I'm bringing home this weekend, help me with my essay and iron my shirts?' Surely this form of slavery qualifies for at least a small measure of greatness!

Unfortunately there is more to it than that. When the disciples bickered about who was to be the greatest in the kingdom of God, Jesus told them this upside-down order of the servant being the greatest. He acted this out in a way they would never forget when he washed their feet—the master of the universe taking the role of a nobody. What is more, Jesus washed the feet of the people he knew would abandon him, even betray him, in just a short while. He acted from a position of strength, not responding to a demand from the disciples but choosing to shock them by his generous self-giving.

Jack, aged 70, used to nod to his neighbour Ben over the garden fence. One day Ben confided that his wife was ill, so he didn't have anyone to go out with any more. Jack asked Ben if he would like to go with him to the over-60s club, but didn't admit that he had always avoided going there himself. One day Ben said he might like to go to church, so Jack stopped going to the church he usually attended in order to take Ben to their village church. Now they go together every week.

Each time, Jack had helped without Ben ever realizing that it had involved some sacrifice. Like a good servant, Jack had anticipated Ben's needs and, to Ben, Jack was the greatest gift he could have had.

Is there someone you can serve today without them noticing?

WP

Let's be honest

For all who exalt themselves will be humbled, and those who humble themselves will be exalted.

Here Jesus uses the example of a wedding guest choosing where to sit to illustrate how important it is to have a realistic view of ourselves in God's kingdom. The guest confidently placed himself up near the high table, only to be removed to a lower seat by the host when a more important person arrived. The social setting was being used by the guest as a way to impress others and to boost his ego.

We may think that we don't do this, but it can creep in ever so subtly. I am obsessed with gardening, and I sometimes hear myself saying things like 'Isn't the *Thalictrum aquilegiifolium* looking good?' What?! Surely my listener would have been happier with 'tall purple fluffy stuff'. Am I displaying my knowledge because the other person wants to know or because I'm showing off?

If we exalt ourselves, we are automatically demoting others. Give us a little bit of power and we can all be guilty of misusing it. There is nothing wrong with power used sensibly but it should not be a means of building our own egos. Look out for the traps! There are people like me, who find delegation difficult. Is that because we are silently claiming that only we can do it right? Is there a temptation to run other people's lives for them because we think our way is best? Is it easy to spot other people's failings and make the most of them, making us look good in comparison? Do we reject other people's ideas simply because they are different from ours?

We are all called to become the very best we can be. A good first step is to acknowledge that we are not as good as we pretend we are, and to ask for God's forgiveness. Then, in God's upside-down kingdom, the gracious host can reassure us that in his eyes we are simply great!

Lord, help us to exalt you, not ourselves.

WP

James 1:19–27 (NIV)

What is community?

Do not merely listen to the word, and so deceive yourselves.
Do what it says.

'Community' is a fashionable concept. It is especially prominent among the advocates of postmodern philosophy. Trying to get a grip on postmodernity is like trying to catch eels in a wet meadow in the dark—not something I have tried, but I know it is quite an art. One thing that is clear, however, is the difference in emphasis that modernity and postmodernity put on 'creed' and 'community'.

Let us put it more simply. When I was a child and the world was still 'modern', the emphasis was on what you believed. As long as you believed the right things, you were OK—no one was going to make too many demands on how you lived. You could live in glorious isolation, and people did. Now I find myself as an adult in the postmodern world where the emphasis is not on what you believe, but on what you do; as long as you do what is acceptable within your chosen community, what you believe is irrelevant as long as you relate.

In today's world, most people base their lives on relationships: living in communities that are defined by common lifestyles, acted out in mutually accepted, but often transient, codes of behaviour. But these relationships are not based on mutual beliefs.

Stop and think about it for a minute. Neither of these options is actually acceptable for the follower of Jesus Christ. Jesus didn't tell us to believe the right things and carry on regardless, and he didn't tell us to live a certain way and believe what we like. Jesus emphasized both right belief and right action. Right belief spurs on right action, and right action flows from, and is reinforced by, right belief. You cannot have one without the other—if you want to follow Jesus.

Lord, help me to get the right grip on what you mean by true community and use that understanding to challenge the spirit of the age in word and action.

AS

A communal God

Then God said, 'Let us make man in our image, in our likeness, and let them rule over the fish of the sea and the birds of the air, over the livestock, over all the earth, and over all the creatures that move along the ground.'

We have gone back to the beginning of the Bible today, to try to find out why relationship or community is so important to human beings. Today's verses have been the root of an incredible amount of discussion throughout the history of biblical interpretation—but I want to look at them today from a purely devotional point of view.

The thing that is commonly pointed out about these verses is that, in the original Hebrew text, and thus in translation, God refers to himself in the plural; he uses the pronouns 'us' and 'our' when he declares his intention to create humans in the image of God. This use of plural pronouns is not like the royal 'we', used by our Queen when addressing the nation—it really does imply that God considers himself in the plural! This continues throughout the Old Testament; whenever we read the name Lord, we are reading a singular representation of a plural Jewish word: Elohim.

Christians have used these verses in Genesis and the plural nature of God to develop the teaching on the Trinity—that of God as Father, Son and Holy Spirit. God is a communal God; although he is one, he is also a unity of personalities in perfect relationship.

If we are made in the image of a God who is communal in nature, then we are going to be the same—communal in nature. The desire for relationship and to live in community is part of the hereditary make up we have been given by our creator.

Lord, you have made us to desire relationship—with you and with other people. Please bring us to a fuller understanding of what you intend that to mean.

AS

The author of community

*The Lord God said, 'It is not good for the man to be alone.
I will make a helper suitable for him.'*

Although it is beyond our comprehension for an individual to be one and many at the same time, the Bible clearly represents God like that. The fact that this sort of comprehension is beyond us, indicates that human beings may have been made in God's image, but they are not perfect copies. Human beings were created as individuals; there is only one of us in each body. We don't experience the same kind of inner relationship with a significant other self in the way that God does.

God looked at the being he had made and realized that the deep inner communal characteristic of himself was incomplete. Maybe it was intentional—we are told God intended to make a human being not another divine one. How was God to satisfy the latent need for relationship that his imprint had left in the being he had made? God decided to make more than one; and not just more than one, but a different sort, so that their interaction could in some way recapture the intimacy and closeness that God himself experienced in his own communal nature. That is where woman came into the picture.

Was Adam actually masculine before Eve was created? Did God have more remodelling to do than a basic rib transplant? Sexual difference must have been God's intention at some stage, as he had already created plants and animals that way. It could be that God decided that this was the best way to recapture the communal nature of himself in purely physical bodies that lacked true divinity.

Eve as Adam's 'helper' can be seen in a completely different light, when considered from the perspective of God trying to recreate his communal nature. From this perspective, Eve is one of two equal beings whose mutual interaction helps each counterpart to discover and experience the relational nature of the creator God.

Ask God to show you what intimacy and closeness can mean.

                                                                    AS

Rules for community

I am the Lord your God... showing love to a thousand generations of those who love me and keep my commandments.

Having spent a couple of days in the Garden of Eden, it is time for us to move on. As we all know, Adam and Eve made a mess of their potential for relationship with God by disobeying his command. Their loss of innocence and their being thrown out of the Garden is a picture of how human beings are thrown out of relationship with God and with each other as a result of that initial act of disobedience.

Adam and Eve were equally to blame for what happened—he was with her when she picked the fruit (Genesis 3:6). Loss of relationship with God and each other is something that we all need to take responsibility for, we cannot pass the buck to the next person or the opposite sex.

The Bible story tells us that life was not easy for people after Eden. Relationships were dominated by human self-interest, with the usual emphases on accumulating possessions, sexual prowess and secular power. Eventually God decided that the only way to help people learn to live in the kind of communal relationship he had initially intended was to give guidelines and boundaries to help them. Thus we come to today's reading in which Moses tells the people of Israel the commandments that God has given them for successful relational living with the Lord and each other.

Take some time to read through the Ten Commandments as presented in today's reading. Prayerfully consider each one—remind yourself what the boundaries are for living God's way.

Lord, thank you that you are a loving Father and that you have set boundaries within which we can enjoy healthy relationship with you and each other. Forgive us for the times we have stepped beyond the line, deliberately or unintentionally. By your grace, help us to live as you intended.

AS

The triple-braided cord

*Two are better than one, because they have good return for their
work: if one falls down his friend can help him up! ...
Though one may be overpowered, two can defend themselves.
A cord of three strands is not quickly broken.*

This passage is one that is often read during wedding ceremonies; it
is a very good illustration of how husband and wife, as a nuclear
community, can work in relationship to mutual benefit. In the context of marriage, the cord of three strands is often taken as an illustration of how a marriage is strengthened through difficult times if
God is at the centre. If you are married, take some time to think
about the implications of verses 9–12 for your marriage.

However, if we look at the wider context of verses 9–12, we see
that marriage was not the initial springboard for the thoughts
behind them. Verse 7 tells us that 'there was a man all alone; he had
neither son nor brother'. We could just as easily read any noun, masculine or feminine, for 'man', 'son' or 'brother'.

The key here is that we have a person who is all alone. This person has no rest; their work is never done; everything they do or put
aside is for no ultimate reason. Even without the individual's selfish
intentions, such an existence is seen as meaningless. People are not
designed to operate alone, there is enjoyment and meaning in working with and relating to others with the aim of mutual blessing.

Don't get hung up on verse 11—it can be taken literally or
metaphorically. You don't need to be married to experience the
warmth and the 'good return' that two people have when they work
or live in a right and healthy relationship with each other—and the
key to healthy relationships is the third strand of the cord—keeping
God at the centre.

---

*Lord, be at the centre of all my relationships, strengthening them
according to your design.*

AS

A commanded blessing

How good and pleasant it is when brothers live together in unity!
... For there the Lord bestows his blessing, even life for evermore.

The people of Israel sang this psalm when they processed up to the temple in Jerusalem to worship the Lord. On such days, the people were united in worship as they gathered to consecrate themselves to God. The real challenge, however, was to take the blessing of that unity back into their ordinary lives in the community.

The unity that God intended to be characteristic of his people in the ordinary place as well as in the gathered place is described as being like oil that is used to anoint the head and is running down into Aaron's beard. This refers to Aaron's anointing as Israel's high priest (Exodus 30:22–33). It indicates that when unity is centred on seeking to put God first in a community, that community is consecrated in such a way that God commands his blessing to fall upon them (cf. Numbers 6:22–26).

The unity God desired for his people is also compared to the dew that comes down on Mount Hermon—but note, here this dew actually falls on Mount Zion, the place where the people gather to worship the Lord. Unity in the place where the people gather to worship is like dew, which comes down and nourishes and causes growth, which should sustain that unity in everyday circumstances.

When a community of people is committed to consecrating themselves for the Lord's purposes and to worshipping him, unity is a natural consequence. The blessings that come from unity in the gathered place extend into the everyday life of the community, so that the people can live in unity as well as worshipping in unity. This is 'good and pleasant' for those who experience it and attractive for those who see it in action.

Thank you, Lord, that when we seek your face as a community of your people, you give us a double blessing—both good and pleasant—that follows us into our everyday lives and marks them out for you.

AS

Jesus redefines community

My command is this: Love each other as I have loved you.
Greater love has no one than this, that he lay down
his life for his friends.

When Jesus taught about how God expected people to live in community with each other, he lifted what people believed but didn't necessarily do to a whole new level of understanding. He explained the Jewish law and the Ten Commandments in a way that left people unable to continue seeing these laws as decoration, and helped them to realize that what we believe has implications for our relationships with each other in thought and action, not just in principle.

You can find Jesus' ideals for community living in Matthew 5—7, but in today's passage in John's Gospel we read about how Jesus feels about people who don't unite inner belief with outward action; people who don't bear fruit for the kingdom of God by living in 'community' with him and showing that in the way they relate to others. People who don't abide in Jesus will not bear fruit. They will wither and find themselves cut of from the kingdom. It is hard stuff, but a stern reminder that Christians don't function well on their own under normal circumstances.

Jesus then gives his disciples a new commandment that sums up everything he has ever taught them: love each another as I have loved you. For Jesus, to love as he loves is to be willing to sacrifice oneself entirely for another person—he asks no more than he has willingly done himself.

Living in community with others would be impossible without self-sacrifice of all kinds. Some of the biggest sacrifices made on behalf of others are the accumulation of many small sacrifices made on a daily basis. Even the smallest act of love is not wasted when it comes to oiling relationships.

Lord, I'm not very good at loving as you want me to. Fill me again with your love, so that I can put other people first with an attitude that brings glory to your name.

AS

The fellowship of believers

*They devoted themselves to the apostles' teaching... to the
breaking of bread and to prayer... All the believers were together
and had everything in common.*

In the beginning of Acts, we see how the first Christians interpreted
and lived out Jesus' new commandment to love one another. Most
of them were new converts; around 3000 people! We read that all
these new believers were together; they were devoted to hearing the
teaching of Jesus from the apostles (Matthew 28:20), remembering
Jesus in the breaking of bread (Matthew 14:19) and in prayer (Luke
18:1). The physical experience of Jesus was fresh in people's minds,
and they wanted to live in relationship with him and each other in
the way he had commanded the disciples.

It cannot have been physically possible for all 3000 to be all
together all of the time, but we do read that they were 'together'.
Even if they met in smaller groups, they were together in purpose
and showed that intent in their devotion to learning about Jesus and
worshipping him, whether at home or in the temple. Such devotion
and worship couldn't do anything other than spill over into radical
action in the case of these new believers. They took the content
of the Sermon on the Mount seriously and began to share their
possessions in a radical way, selling things they owned to provide for
other believers' needs.

I don't think that the first believers' radical experiment in 'community' living meant that they all moved into one large house and
lived from a common purse, but they certainly looked out for each
other with a sense of self-sacrifice that we find hard to match in
contemporary society.

What marks out the Christian 'communities' we live in from any
other 'community' in secular society? Can people say of our church,
'Look, how these Christians love one another!' because they see
material sacrifice turning into love in action? Is there anyone who
needs your help?

Lord, open my eyes, open my heart and then open my hands.

AS

One body, many parts

*The body is a unit, though it is made up of many parts; and
though all its parts are many, they form one body... Now you are
the body of Christ, and each one of you is a part of it.*

I once read about a university lecturer who asked his students how
many of them knew the name of the crippled old woman who
mopped the corridors of the department. Not one of them raised
their hand. One student, however, took the challenge to heart and
made it her particular concern to find out the name of the old
cleaner and befriend her. She did so—and subsequently greeted the
woman by name each time they met, often taking time to chat. The
change in the old woman became noticeable; she straightened her
back, began to smile and talk to the other students. The student,
who initially befriended the woman, went on to become successful
in business and put her success down to learning to value every person, however lowly, in her large organization.

There is a real lesson here for those of us who belong to church
communities. In every church, there are people who don't seem
attractive, have strange habits or do jobs that are not in the spotlight. Why do we shy away from such people: it isn't fear, it is
actually pride. Paul tells us that all the parts of Christ's body, the
Church, are equally important and should have equal concern for
each other (v. 25). Some people do need to be treated with special
consideration (v. 23), but that doesn't mean they need to be
ignored!

Take some time to think about the people in your congregation
that you instinctively shy away from. Ask yourself why you do that.
Ask the Lord to deal with any root issues in your life that make you
shun people who need special consideration. Sometimes all it takes
is a smile to start a process that allows a person to blossom.

Lord, you had time for outcasts, give me time for them, too.

AS

Doing good to all

Let us not become weary in doing good, for at the proper time we will reap a harvest if we do not give up. Therefore, as we have opportunity, let us do good to all people, especially those who belong to the family of believers.

Paul's letters to the young churches give us practical instruction about how to live out Jesus' command to love one another. The first step to loving like Jesus is to learn humility. Only when people are truly humble, and consider others better than themselves, can people submit to one another in love and do good to one another in the loving way Christ intended.

Humility comes from being given the spiritual insight to see yourself as you really are. When we come to realize our total dependence on Christ for everything that we are in God, then our gifts and capabilities, which can be used to help others, can be considered in their right perspective. If we refuse to lay down our pride, we deceive ourselves (v. 3) and really need to test the motives we have for the 'good' things we might be doing for others. If we are humble and loving, then helping others to carry the things that weigh them down is not the difficulty it might otherwise be.

Paul encourages us in this letter to carry each other's burdens. We can do that in prayer by praying for those who are too burdened to pray for themselves. We carry one another's burdens in action with a well-timed offer of help. We can also help others lay down some burdens by taking time to be trustworthy listeners who are willing to minister healing prayer to people's hearts and minds.

All the time, though, we are told to keep a watch on ourselves. There is no place for complacency in a community of believers, we are all only human after all—and it could be our turn to receive help next!

Lord, you are good to all. Help me to be the same.

AS

Be careful how you live

But among you there must not be even a hint of sexual immorality, or of any kind of impurity, or of greed, because these things are improper for God's holy people.

In this passage, Paul tells the believers to imitate God and live a life of love because Christ loved them and gave himself up for them. Then he immediately brings them down to earth by saying that a community of believers must not allow the smallest hint of sexual misconduct to enter into their relationships with each other. Such behaviour is improper and, when it does happen, it brings the name of Christ into disrepute.

As a church leader's wife, I have seen numerous occasions when church members have naively laid themselves open to criticism of sexual misconduct by not thinking ahead, even when their actual behaviour has been faultless. All it takes is a car parked in someone else's drive too late at night and only once, never mind once too often, for people in a local community to start talking. The problem that many right-living Christians face is that they are so right-living that they can't see how some of the innocent things they do can be misinterpreted! Even taking a box of bottles to the recycling bin can raise eyebrows. It doesn't matter that it took twelve months to fill the box—only that it is full!

The other problem some Christians face is that they can believe that everyone else in their Christian community has the same lovingly policed moral boundaries as they have. It is only when it is too late that they realize their actions have been misinterpreted by someone who is having problems maintaining their own boundaries or who has no concept of boundaries at all.

Any relationship within a community can be a minefield of potential disasters if we haven't taken time to know our own limits, understand other people's limits, think ahead and keep prayerfully alert.

Search me, O God, and know my heart… see if there is any offensive way in me, and lead me in the way everlasting.

AS

Love with actions

*Dear children, let us not love with words or tongue but with
actions and in truth.*

It is quite incredible how many times in the New Testament the call
to love each other as Christ loved us and laid down his life for us is
followed by a very practical application. Today's reading is no excep-
tion and the exhortation to love each other is followed by a rhetor-
ical question that demands we answer it by saying, 'No, God's love
cannot be in a person who sees a brother in material need and walks
by without doing anything about it.'

As a clergy family, we have often been on the receiving end of
people whose love for God has been expressed in material action. I
remember bags of groceries appearing on the doorstep after we had
received an unexpected tax demand that wiped out our housekeep-
ing for half of April one year. Again, an unexpected cheque arrived
when our dog needed an expensive emergency operation. We all
appreciate being on the receiving end, but in the economy of the
kingdom of God, you are more blessed when you give. Knowing the
love Jesus has for us should spur all of us to equally generous acts of
kindness as the ones we have received.

Often the opportunity to give comes when we all least expect it.
I remember making friends with a woman who was new to the country. Then one morning I received a phone call from her—she and
her young family had been thrown out of their lodgings into the
pouring rain—could I help? Eventually they were rehoused, but the
flat was empty of all but a bed. I am still amazed at the number of
times I have shared the contents of my kitchen cupboards, larder
and airing cupboard with people to find that all my cupboards are
still full.

---

*Give, and it will be given to you... for with the measure you use, it
will be measured to you (Luke 6:38). Help me today, Lord, to put this
verse to the test.*

                                                                    AS

The call to persevere

Let us not give up meeting together, as some are in the habit of doing, but let us encourage one another—and all the more as you see the Day approaching.

Being part of a vibrant community isn't always easy. There are times when we want to lock the door, shut the curtains and pretend we are not at home. Wanting to spend time alone or with the ones you love isn't wrong in itself—time for recuperation and refreshment can be very necessary when we have overdone things—but followers of Jesus cannot abdicate entirely from being in relationship with a Christian community, especially when they are going through tough times. We all need each other.

When a coal falls out of the fire, it soon goes out. It is the same with our Christian faith and lifestyle—remove yourself from a Christian church or community, and your faith begins to waver and the lifestyle begins to slip. We need to meet together with each other on a regular basis if we are to keep our faith alive and our lives up to scratch.

Persevering with meeting together isn't always easy. Last week, the person leading the service in our church innocently asked the congregation to volunteer reasons why they were there that morning. I slipped behind my notice sheet and hoped he wouldn't see me—I wasn't there for any good reason other than plain obedience; the human side of me would rather have been at home having an hour's peace and quiet. There are times when we have to turn out for a meeting out of pure obedience, because we know that staying at home would be the first step down a slippery slope to persistent absenteeism and a backsliding faith.

Being a Christian isn't always about warm feelings and celebration; sometimes it can just be a matter of perseverance and self-discipline until our feelings catch up with our heads again.

Lord, I don't want to neglect meeting with other Christians—help me when it feels difficult.

AS

The heavenly community

Now the dwelling of God is with men, and he will live with them. They will be his people, and God himself will be with them and be their God. He will wipe every tear from their eyes.

It is getting to be quite an old joke now, when the preacher says to the congregation, 'You'd better get used to the people in the pews around you, because you'll be seeing a lot of them in heaven', but he is absolutely right! Everything we go through here on earth is preparing us for eternal life with God in heaven, and nothing sharpens us up more than learning to live in community with many Christians who can be just as awkward and imperfect as we are!

It is hard for us to imagine what relationships will be like in heaven. We know that Jesus said there would be no marriage (Matthew 22:30), so intimacy in relationships will be on a completely unknown level.

Today's passage tells us there will be no more tears, so the pain we expose ourselves to when we risk reaching out to others will not be a factor in heaven—there will be no more misunderstanding, no more potential to accidentally offend and hurt others. I can tell you, I am looking forward to that bit!

The thing that makes it clear that the new heavenly community will be completely beyond anything we have ever experienced is that God will make his dwelling with us and live with us: he himself will be with us (v. 3b). I don't think that this is just a restoration of the relationship with God that Adam and Eve lost in the Garden of Eden, but something even higher and more special; perhaps something like the incomprehensible singular yet plural nature of God himself that we thought about two weeks ago. Whatever it is, it is worth waiting for and working for—I hope I get to see you there!

Thank you, Lord, for the hope that you have given us—hope of an eternity spent with you.

AS

The power of God

Great is our Lord and mighty in power;
his understanding has no limits.

This has been an exciting time for me as I have studied the Psalms once again—it is indeed a book of worship. A hymnbook and a him-book—it is all about the Lord. The Psalms record deep devotions and dark dejection. They speak to us, and often for us, as they contain every experience we face and express, not only praise and worship in a way I never could, but also I find an echo in my heart as I read David's prayers and cries to the Lord. Someone once said, 'The book of Psalms instructs us in the use of wings as well as words. It sets us both mounting and singing.'

In the coming days, as we look at Psalms together, I hope you will again see the power of God in your life. His power won't diminish or destroy you but will, I pray, encourage you to see again his attention to detail in all you face—and his delight in you as a unique part of his creation.

It is my prayer that you will see that you can trust God, because he really is all-powerful—but he doesn't abuse his power because alongside his power is his mercy and his grace. There is power enough in God to help the weakest of us and grace enough to help the unworthiest of us.

We can often be so afraid of those who feel they exert some power over us, such is the rush to gain as much power as possible in the workplace and, dare I say, in some churches. This form of power is always destructive. It is humans' effort at power, not the example the Lord gives us and displays all around us and within each of us as we allow him access to our lives.

In the coming days, we shall explore the many facets of God's unique power.

Father, we stand in awe of your power—you are majestic in all your ways. Reveal your power again today.

SW

The power of God—to create

By the word of the Lord were the heavens made, their starry host by the breath of his mouth.

I have no problem in looking at the world around me and giving the glory and recognition to God for all he has done. I do believe that he is that powerful and really did create the heavens and the earth! Am I being too simplistic? We have become so sophisticated with space exploration that the creation story of a God who brought the world into being by the 'breath of his mouth' is considered myth.

We do have a wealth of knowledge and information at our fingertips, which distracts us from the Genesis account of creation. Instead of an all-powerful, big God we have the Big Bang theory: the universe and all we see came into being almost by chance in a haphazard sort of way.

Recently I looked at some information regarding this unique planet of ours and became even more convinced that we are indeed part of God's wonderfully creative plan. The earth is tilted at an angle of 23.5 degrees. It rotates on its axis at about 700 miles per hour. If it were to rotate at even one-tenth of its present rate then all plant life would be burnt to a crisp during the day or frozen at night! At the same time as it rotates, it also orbits the sun at 18.5 miles a second ecliptically, which gives us our seasons. The sun is set at 93 million miles from us—any closer and we would burn up in its intense heat, any further away and our eco-structure would disintegrate.

Such precision speaks to me of a powerful creator whose eye for detail and delight in all he created didn't stop there. He chose to share it with you and me, not to diminish his power but to display it through us!

Father, the detail and precision of creation are incredible—I stand in awe of you!

SW

The power of God to create—us!

When I consider your heavens, the work of your fingers,
the moon and the stars, which you have set in place,
what is man that you are mindful of him?

Do you ever take time 'to consider the heavens' and all the Lord
has created?

Some years ago, I watched the sunset over the Grand Canyon.
I may never see it again so I begged the friends I was travelling with
to stay and watch. Crowds gathered; anticipation and expectation
rose as the sun gradually disappeared. The sky was ablaze with pinks
and purples and golds—each colour taking its turn to bathe the
Canyon in its particular hue. Silence reigned as the sun left the
scene and it seemed all of creation held its breath, totally awestruck
at this display of God's creative power. Some people in the crowd
applauded—I cried. As I remember that scene and then look at my
life, I wonder like David: 'what is man that you are mindful of him?'

As David walked one night, his gaze went heavenwards—did he
wonder not only at the 'how' of creation, but the 'why'?

We are told in Genesis 1 that after God created the heavens and
the earth, the light, dark, the water, land, vegetation and the animals, he created us. We were the last on his creative list (Genesis
1:26–28). We are the pinnacle of God's creation! We are unique in
the way we relate and respond to him—we are distinguished from
the beasts as most of them are formed to look downward to the
earth—but you and I are made erect to look upwards towards
heaven!

God's power to create has a purpose—you and I were created to
know him and make him known. His power, immense as it is, is also
gentle and precise. His is the power to create... and relate.

There is power enough in God to help the weakest and grace
enough to help the unworthiest.

Read Psalm 8 again as a prayer.

SW

The power of God—in history

One generation will commend your works to another...
They will tell of the power of your awesome works...

If you have some time, do read Psalm 105 and 106. You will find a
succinct history of the people of Israel and the Lord's dealing and
intervention with them. From the time of Abraham and beyond,
they detail the powerful intervention of God in the history of this
nation. It is not only the history of the nation of Israel—it is also
God's story... his-story!

I love to read the familiar stories and to be reminded of not only
what God has done—but to be challenged to believe in what he can
still do today. I wonder what our generation will commend to the
next as far as telling of the power of God's awesome works. In telling
his-story do we add our story, too?

We have the same experiences as those famed and flawed individuals we are told about in the Bible.

Have you ever felt like Abraham—being asked to leave all you
were familiar with to go to a land you didn't know? Have you ever
felt as Joseph did as he was wrongly accused and incarcerated for a
crime he didn't commit, but who could later say to his brothers, 'You
intended to harm me, but God intended it for good...' (Genesis
50:19–20).

Do you have experiences that can be likened to Moses and the
burning bush? Have you had a life-changing encounter with God
that burned within your heart and changed the course of your life
for eternity? Have you experienced his daily provision of manna as
you have wandered in a wilderness place?

What is your story of your encounters with God that can be told
to those around you—to the next generation? You are history in
the making—your life tells a unique, story too, and will display the
power of his awesome works.

---

*Father, help us to tell our story and 'commend you' to those around
us today.*

                                                              SW

The power of God—to protect

*If you make the Most High your dwelling... then no harm will
befall you, no disaster will come near your tent...*

This beautiful psalm speaks of God's protection of us. We can rest
in his shadow and be covered by his 'feathers and find refuge under
his wings'. I find I need the protection of his shadow and the comfort of knowing his 'feathers' are around me each day.

The world around us can be a fearful place. Because of my wheelchair, I may seem more 'vulnerable' than most, yet I have never
been conscious of it—until recently.

I live in a small bungalow beside a community centre and a small
church. Each Friday evening the community centre has been a mag-
net for scores of teenagers to gather and make merry (among other
things!) A few weeks ago, as the numbers increased so did the noise
and the damage—I have learned that reasoning with the group only
produces more noise, damage and abuse and makes me feel very vulnerable! So I phoned the police. The officer I spoke to was kind and
assured me of their help. As I apologized for calling, she said, 'Don't
worry, it is what we are here for.'

As I hung up, I realized that there are so many situations in my
life that are too big or dangerous for me to deal with, but the Lord
has the power to protect me. It is what he is here to do for us. Just
as I couldn't do a thing about the huge gang of youths but needed
to call for help and protection, he knows the situations I find myself
in that are beyond my capabilities. He answers my call and lets
me know again and again that he is there to 'cover me with his
feathers' and allow me to find refuge and safety in his care.

---

*Look at Isaiah 43:1–2 and let its promise of protection remind you of
God's power when you feel vulnerable.*

SW

The power of God—to judge

He will judge the world in righteousness;
he will govern the peoples with justice...

God's acts of judgment are easily seen in the Old Testament—the flood, the destruction of Sodom and Gomorrah, the plagues upon Egypt, and so on. David will have been familiar with God's intervention on behalf of the people of Israel and the judgments meted out on their enemies. Sometimes the Old Testament can read as a record of harsh judgment!

The New Testament also has instances of the Lord judging wrongdoing—Ananias and Sapphira and Simon the Sorcerer (Acts 5 and 8:9–25). The history of God's dealings with Israel and the early Church are often spoken of as 'salvation history'—and are a visual aid showing who he is by the way he acts. The wonderful thing this side of Calvary is that God's character hasn't changed— but his solution has now been revealed!

Does that make it easier for us to understand that he still has the power to judge, or do we see him as kind and gracious—a God who wouldn't dare declare war on our feelings and actions?

If I witness what I perceive to be wrongdoing and injustice, my reactions can sometimes be less than gracious. Recently I found myself in a situation where my initial reaction was to be angered by things being said about me. Initially I thought of asking the Lord to visit a plague upon my accusers, but with the help of godly friends, I stepped back and took time to try to understand why the situation had arisen. In the process, I learned more about myself and the areas in my life the Lord does want to deal with and heal. I discovered, again, that I have no right to judge others. When I judge, I usurp a divine function and step into areas of people's lives and behaviour where I have no right to go.

Father, you see more than I ever can. You know more than I ever will.
Judgment is yours not mine.

                                                                    SW

The power of God—to vindicate

Vindicate me, O Lord, for I have led a blameless life;
I have trusted in the Lord without wavering.

Few of us will experience the horrors David faced. He was hunted and hounded. His life and reputation were in danger many times as he ran from not only King Saul's attempts to kill him but also the cruel slanders hurled in his direction.

I often fall into the trap of being quick to judge. I jump quickly to the defence of friends I feel have been treated less than favourably, but, just as God has the power to judge, he has the wisdom and insight to vindicate… and the means.

I have realized the little adage 'sticks and stones may break my bones but words will never harm me' is rubbish! Give me the sticks and stones any day, rather than some of the things I hear said about people.

Recently a very close friend experienced and bore out this verse. Initially I was there as the 'ferocious and loyal terrier' another friend called me! But I soon realized that the Lord didn't need my help to defend or vindicate her. The situation was horrendous and, sadly, involved other Christians whom I valued and respected. As my friend patiently and graciously listened, however, allowing the accusations to come, it was evident that those who had whispered in secret didn't have the courage to speak in the open. Mountains had been made out of molehills and, as I watched and prayed, I saw Jesus stand alongside my friend as he had with the woman in John 8—the situation wasn't as serious but soon her accusers left the scene, too.

It is right sometimes for us to defend a person or a cause we feel passionately about, but, without fail, it is the Lord who vindicates and defends in a way we never could or should. Sometimes we see him in action. Most times, we have to wait for years to see that he has defended our lives and defended his name.

Make verses 2 and 3 your prayer today.

                                                                    SW

The power of God—to hear

*I love the Lord, for he heard my voice; he heard my
cry for mercy. Because he turned his ear to me, I will call upon
him as long as I live.*

If someone asked you why you love the Lord, what would your
response be? 'I love the Lord because…'

Years ago, I heard a man share his wartime experiences in the
Blitz. He told of the time his home was destroyed and he was buried
under the rubble crying out for help, not sure that his voice could
be heard above the noise of bombs dropping all over London. It was,
and he was rescued. Someone had been trained to listen out for
cries for help.

Who hears our voice today? Do we feel as if our voice is drowned
out by the noises around us—or others in far deeper need? We do
need to know that our voice, and most importantly our prayers, are
being heard; that God is still turning his ear towards us and listening to even the faintest prayer.

These days one problem I do find difficult to cope with (apart
from my obvious mobility ones!) is that if I am in a room full of people chattering to one another or even alongside others talking, I find
it almost impossible to filter out the 'background chatter' and con-
centrate on the conversation I am supposed to be having. It is the
same in those little 'get-together-in-small-groups-and-pray' times
we often have at church. How my heart sinks! Yet without fail in the
midst of such noise and distractions if someone calls my name I
hear—especially if it is a familiar voice calling.

I know the Lord has the power to hear my voice above the clam-
our of the world; above the noise of countless billions of others calling. He has the power to hear me when I call his name.

---

*Psalm 34:15 says 'his ears are attentive to their cry'. He bends low to
hear our whispered prayers. Call out to him today.*

                                                        SW

The power of God—to forgive

Have mercy on me, O God, according to your unfailing love;
according to your great compassion blot out my transgressions.
Wash away all my iniquity and cleanse me from my sin.

This psalm conveys the depth of David's remorse over his sin—he recognizes that it is against God that he has sinned and only to God that he can come for cleansing and forgiveness. David realizes that it isn't a burnt offering God wants, but a broken and contrite heart. This psalm is written from brokenness and contrition.

When I fail and fall, and am so conscious of the sin in my life, I use this psalm as a framework for prayer. Like David I am aware that I need the mercy of God and his forgiveness—aware that even those sins I think are hidden are known to God. I ask him to 'create in me a clean heart'.

The word used for 'create' is the same as in Genesis 1. Just as God created the heavens and the earth out of a void, he creates a clean heart from the 'nothing' I bring him and gives the opportunity for a new start, a new beginning.

His power to forgive is awesome. He could easily annihilate us; he could refuse and give us what we deserve; but the same God, who has the power to judge, has the power to forgive. Do we accept it— and, in accepting, do we forgive ourselves? When I have been in need of forgiveness from the Lord and others, I can come to that place of acceptance, of realizing he forgives me, and that others do too. But I often struggle with forgiving myself.

If you are struggling today to accept forgiveness, use this psalm as your prayer. He will answer and will create a clean heart in you, restoring to you the joy of his salvation. He did it for David. He does it for me. He will do it for you.

Use this psalm as your prayer for today.

SW

The power of God—to love

Give thanks to the Lord, for he is good. His love endures for ever.

There are 26 verses in this psalm—and 26 responses with the same words: 'His love endures for ever'. When I read this psalm recently, I wondered if I could chart a path through my history as this psalm does and after each 'episode' say, 'His love endures for ever'.

Here are some of mine. Why not try this for yourself and insert your own episodes. It is an encouragement and a challenge. It has helped me to see again that nothing will or ever can separate me from his love as Romans 8:38–39 wonderfully says. His love is directed towards us personally. He loves you with an enduring, steadfast love.

- *Accepting Jesus as my Saviour and Lord. His love endures for ever.*
- *My younger brother's birth when I was 16. His love endures for ever.*
- *My younger brother telling me he was gay on his 21st birthday. His love endures for ever.*
- *All the years of my nursing career. His love endures for ever.*
- *Working in Africa as a missionary seeing abject poverty and need. His love endures for ever.*
- *Working with families of disabled children, being present at their birth and sometimes their death. His love endures for ever.*
- *Sitting with a young woman as her pregnancy was terminated because the baby was profoundly disabled. His love endures for ever.*
- *The diagnosis of multiple sclerosis. His love endures for ever.*
- *Losing my job, my house, some friends. His love endures for ever.*
- *New challenges, new friends, new opportunities to make him known. His love endures for ever.*
- *Periods of darkness and illness with no end in sight. His love endures for ever.*
- *A sure hope of my future in heaven. His love endures for ever.*

My list goes on, but each day I know his love endures all of my doubts and my fears.

May this be your experience of him today: his love for you endures for ever!

SW

The power of God—to know

O Lord, you have searched me and you know me.

I read this psalm when I need to know that he really does know all about me; does care deeply for me; and loves me... despite myself! Yet the realization that God is omniscient may bring a sense of terror—can he really know everything about me? Does he see me in all the dark places I think I can hide from him? Was he really there knitting me together before I was born?

Rather than terrifying me this psalm brings me comfort. This damaged body of mine is known through and through by him—even the likes of me are fearfully and wonderfully made (v. 14).

What does it mean for our all-powerful, all-knowing God to search and know us? One way I have of understanding this is to look at my life as belonging to a different 'landlord'. At one time the 'landlord' I had was the devil—he was mean and evil. He would come along and wander through the 'rooms' of my life telling me what a mess I was in! Then one day I met a new landlord—he banished the old one and asked if he could help me—so I invited him into my life.

He didn't force his way in. He never ran roughshod over my life. Sometimes I would try to clean up the mess before he came—but then I remembered that first day and how he cleaned up the mess he found. Now he gently clears and cleans each room. He has even cleaned out the dark attic where I had buried all the bad things of the past... talk about a loft conversion!

He has searched and he knows me... and loves me still.

As we allow him to search us, he does it gently. The handle to each 'room' is on our side of the door. He will not beat the door down—but once allowed in, his touch, his presence, will transform our lives for ever.

Use verses 23–24 as a prayer today.

                                                              SW

The power of God—to understand

My God, my God, why have you forsaken me?

This psalm is usually recognized as a prophetic, messianic psalm; written hundreds of years before Jesus walked the earth. Many of its verses are fulfilled in the Gospel accounts of the crucifixion of Jesus. Verse 1 is spoken by Jesus from the cross in Matthew 27:46.

You and I will never know the total abandonment Jesus experienced—God turned his back on his Son as he bore the sin of the world. I will never understand all he went through and suffered, but he understands all that we go through. He has the power to understand—not only because he is omnipotent, but because he became flesh and dwelt among us. He lived as we do, experienced all we ever could and asked God the same questions many of us try to restrain and hold back from uttering.

'My God, my God, why have you forsaken me?' Have you ever asked that question or found yourself in a situation where it seems as if your prayers bounce back unanswered? Or have you stifled the question and held back from speaking the words for fear of invoking some terrible response from God?

He understands all you face, all you fear, all you wonder and worry about. It isn't wrong or a sin to question God—it isn't a sin to feel forsaken. Often it is those questions that bring the opportunities for God to respond. Sometimes the answers come directly and in ways we can easily understand.

Other times they come in a different guise and something dies before something else can live. Calvary love understands in a way we may never fathom.

David wrote this psalm from the depths of his despair—his anguish was answered and deliverance came. Hundreds of years later a man on a cross uttered the same words—his prayer was answered for you and for me. His abandonment by God means I never will be abandoned. He really does understand.

Thank you, Jesus, for the cross.

                                                              SW

The power of God—to help

I will lift up my eyes to the hills—where does my help come from?
My help comes from the Lord, the Maker of heaven and earth.

What it is about looking to the hills that inspires us to trust him and
receive our help from him. Each time I visit nearby hills or mountains they inspire me and assure me of God's awesome power
through his creation. I see beyond the hills and know that the God
who made them is the one who helps me.

Sometimes asking for help is seen as a weakness. In our self-
sufficient society, we are looked on with some suspicion if we cannot handle or cope with all that life brings. Yet not many of us would
tackle a malfunctioning PC or kitchen appliance—help is on hand,
usually a phone call away, though usually at a price!

Why is it that we can readily accept help for our inanimate
objects but, for this life of ours, we struggle on thinking we should
right the wrongs and be better than we are? Why is it so hard to
admit to God that we still need his help?

Each day I am more and more convinced that all I really do know
is that I don't know! The relief and liberation that brings is wonderful. I am aware of the physical help I need to enable me to function—but spiritually, too. Often all it takes is a glance 'to the hills'
in prayer to alert God to my need.

When the children of Israel were bitten by poisonous snakes
(Numbers 21:4–9) Moses was commanded to make a bronze snake
and put it on a pole. Anyone bitten who looked at the bronze snake
lived… all it took was a glance for them to be healed!

Lord, help me to look to you today. Help me to listen to your voice.
Help me to obey you. Help me to trust you with every detail of my life.
SW

The power of God—to complete

You hem me in—behind and before; you have laid your hand upon me... For you created my inmost being; you knit me together in my mother's womb. I praise you because I am fearfully and wonderfully made.

We often face situations where everything seems to be unravelling before our eyes! Try as we might to keep everything under control, our lives can fall apart at the seams. Many of us will have days when we really do see the edges fray as situations and circumstance take their toll: families to care for; children to ferry to school, then to after-school activities; husbands who need attention and attentiveness; ageing relatives who need practical care. Busy schedules can seem to allow no deviation... or rest! No wonder we fray at the edges!

Yet God has the power to hem us in, to contain, hold us tightly, close to himself so that we don't fall apart. He is the one who began this whole creative process of our lives when he knit us together. He knows what we are made of and knows what to do when the edges fray.

I am left-handed and my mum found it almost impossible to teach me to knit. All I ever seemed to achieve were those little squares that never quite became a blanket—but Mum always had to cast on and cast off! Recently I heard a woman share exactly the same experience! She spoke of our lives being cast on and cast off by God. Each day is a new 'square' in the blanket that becomes our life with its many colours and textures.

Someday he will 'cast off' our lives as we enter eternity complete... our work on earth finished. He has the power to create and to complete each day and every situation. He will make sure that your edges remain secure.

In each of the situations you face today, pray: 'Hem me in today, Lord, and complete your work in me.' Remember, God's Spirit is with you wherever you go.

SW

Journeys—into the unknown

The Lord had said to Abram, 'Leave your country, your people and your father's household and go to the land I will show you.'

Abram is the acclaimed 'Man of Faith'. His name is mentioned not only in the Old Testament but also in all four Gospels, in Acts and also in Paul's letters to Galatia, Corinth and Rome. It was God's covenant with Abraham, as he was to be known, that began the 'special relationship' that moulded a nation and nurtured the faith and education of our Lord Jesus.

Yes, Abram was a colossus, but we seldom pause to look into his life in depth or to recognize that he was by no means on his own— there was a whole family and a wife! Back in the days of around 2000BC, most people were nomadic but there were also city-dwellers, the group to whom Abram obviously belonged. The family had already made the journey from Ur to Haran, some 625 miles north along the river Euphrates, and by Genesis 12, Abram and Co. were enjoying a good life, Haran having accumulated 'many possessions'.

So this bolt out of the blue, this directive from God, must have come as an awful shock to his wife Sarai. Just try to imagine what she must have felt when her husband came into the tent and announced that God had said leave where they were and move on—in faith! Poor Sarai must have had a list of questions buzzing in her mind, but as a wife, and a mere possession, she had no say in the situation.

This part of their journey took them approximately 300 miles down the southern trade routes to Shechem (the present-day city of Nablus), but it wasn't long before they set off once more. This time they trekked south-east towards the Negev Desert. Sarai must have felt she was dropping off the face of the earth!

Lord, help me to follow you willingly. Help me to trust you as you lead me into the unknown.

ER

Moving on again

When Abram came to Egypt, the Egyptians saw that she [Sarai] was a very beautiful woman.

With all the religious works of art to influence our images of biblical characters, we automatically tend to slot Abram and Sarai into 'pensioner' mode. However, the verses recorded in this chapter of Genesis portray a significantly different picture. So attractive was Sarai that Abram felt he had to deceive Pharaoh into thinking she was his sister… a subterfuge that went badly wrong.

The journey through the Negev to Egypt had been shadowed by the fear of famine, a difficult time for catering, yet Sarai survived and retained her attractions; no mean feat after all the stress and hard work of the journey. Egypt was to be a huge test of faith for Sarai, however. Because of Abram's lie she was not protected by a husband and was therefore 'available' to become a tasty addition to Pharaoh's harem.

For the people listening to this story around the ancient camp-fires, this was all compelling stuff! Abram may have been the icon of faith for the men, but Sarai would have been a favourite role model of obedience, resilience and dignity in the face of every adversity. She was a woman of extraordinary faith.

Now there was another journey. When Pharaoh realized the truth, he sent Abram packing, with all the sheep, cattle, donkeys, camels, silver, gold and servants he had acquired during his relatively short stay in the land of Egypt. While the Egyptian experience had tested Sarai to the limit, husband Abram had done well!

We catch such a vivid description of their journey as the author of Genesis recounts them moving 'from place to place' before ending up back near Bethel. These physical journeys were quite enough to cope with but, for Sarai, her journey of faith was just beginning.

Lord, help me to realize that deception has ongoing consequences, often for innocent people. Help me to live a transparent life—an open book where others can see you.

ER

Life's longest journey

'I'm running away from my mistress Sarai,'
she [Hagar] answered.

Here we are face to face with a collision of emotions and cultures. The expectation of all men like Abram was to have a son, the vital component in family continuity. Down in Egypt, he had bought an Egyptian girl and she had journeyed with Abram and Sarai hundreds of miles away from her home and all she understood. The accepted custom was that, if the wife could not bear a son, then a son had to be born from another womb. The accepted custom, yes, but, oh the bitterness and resentment this situation was festering between wife and slave.

It is sometimes said that the longest journey in the world is the nine inches between our head and heart. For Sarai, this was the long, agonizing journey of recognition—she had to swallow the truth that she was barren. To her, it must have seemed that she had failed in her womanhood, she was useless and, in the thinking of those times, worthless.

Let us spare both women a big chunk of our sympathy, Sarai as she rounds on the newly pregnant slave-girl to vent her spite and heartache, and poor Hagar, trapped as the innocent victim in this drama. How desperate the little Egyptian girl must have been to run away in a foreign country; however, she didn't get very far. The 'angel', or 'messenger', from God gave Hagar the comforting promise that she would bear a son, but also urged her to return to Sarai.

When I think of Hagar and Sarai in this eternal triangle, it reminds me of the struggles girls had in Victorian and Edwardian eras—through all the turmoil the women endured, the 'masters' of the house remained frustratingly unconcerned. Was it like this for Sarai and Hagar? What of their equivalents today?

Lord, in my journey to self-discovery, pour the sweet oil of your grace and compassion on the raging waters of my pride and resentment.

ER

God is with us

Where can I go from your Spirit? Where can I flee from your presence?... If I rise on the wings of the dawn, if I settle on the far side of the sea, even there your hand will guide me...

Over the past couple of days, we have been exploring the ripple effects of life's journeys—and each one of us is on a journey. People who have touched our lives most deeply on our journey from help-less baby to adulthood, will have lovingly moulded our attitudes and expectations. For some, the journey through those crucial years has been dominated by fear and trauma, taking years to heal the scars.

The one certainty in life is change! The very word 'journey' implies movement, from one place or experience to another, and at times our confidence evaporates in the face of the unknown. I love to remember what Joyce Grenfell once wrote to a friend: 'Wherever we are, we are always in the same place, in God's hands.' To me, that is Psalm 139 in a nutshell.

Those ancient psalmists were people with the same raw emotions as ourselves, railing at the unfairness of the world and desperate for God's presence and purpose. I find such comfort in these 'Songs of Life', and this psalm in particular reminds me that I am never alone on my journey—today or any other day. In mystery and miracle, God is with me; this almighty creating power of love and life, knows and understands me, accepts and forgives me and is my ever-present guide.

So, on my next journey, whether it takes me to shop, school, office, the hospital, out into the countryside or just to the postbox, God is with me. I can 'walk with him' and 'talk with him' and share my deepest thoughts. This fact should inject my journey today with the 'Wow!' factor.

Thank you, Lord, for keeping me safe in your hands through life's journey. Help me to help others on this pilgrimage with you.

ER

Journey preparation

*These were his [Jesus'] instructions: 'Take nothing for the journey
except a staff—no bread, no bag, no money in your belts. Wear
sandals but not an extra tunic'.*

A young mum I know was saying that Thursday evening was the
only evening when all the family was at home. Otherwise the front
door was constantly banging... journeys to school, from school, to
cubs, drama, choir, rugby training, shopping, the station... six people in a state of perpetual movement. With all these ordinary family
journeys, of course, comes the baggage! The homework, the music
case, pocket money, dinner money, football boots and so on... and
when something gets left behind, a full-scale wobbly erupts.

These are just the daily journeys—how about holidays? Is there
a suitcase on the market that can hold all our immediate necessi-
ties? Have we turned ourselves into such a possession-conscious
culture that too many of us end up going on holiday like demented
hermit crabs weighed down beneath our chosen baggage?

I wonder what Jesus meant when he sent out the disciples? In a
way, he was sending them out without their security blanket of inde-
pendence. They were also going to have to learn the difference
between what they 'wanted' and what they 'needed'. First they
needed to trust him and, in that trust, allow themselves to meet
strangers on an equal basis. They were not to swagger with unnecessary things, nor rely on money to buy influence or clothes to
impress. In other words, they were not going in their own strength
but in the power of the Living God.

It was said that the whole of the United States Congress rose to
greet the tiniest woman who had ever entered the building. She rep-
resented no powerful nation or corporate institution, she owned
nothing but her sari, yet the influence of Mother Teresa's journey
through life has been incalculable.

---

*Lord, help me to jettison my unnecessary baggage so that I am more
able to be open to other people and their needs today.*

ER

Road to recovery

He jumped to his feet and began to walk. Then he went
with them into the temple courts, walking and jumping,
and praising God.

One of the most eagerly awaited journeys is the one that transports
us from sickness back to health; we even use the term 'road to
recovery'.

A few years ago, one of my friends fell through a skylight. When
I visited her in the intensive care unit, the only parts of her body she
could move were her eyelids. It was devastating to see her so completely paralysed, her life apparently ruined by a careless second; her
whole world had crashed. Nothing would ever be the same again.
The future seemed bleak.

I couldn't understand why I felt so shocked. From time to time,
we all hear about people of all ages having terrible accidents but,
until they are known to us personally, the impact is only superficial.
Doreen knew her many friends and church were praying for her and
even groups who only knew her by name added her to their prayer
list. After amazing care from the hospital ICU, she spent six months
at a spinal rehabilitation unit. Here the miracle, which had already
begun, gathered momentum with skilled attention and encouragement. She was thrilled when they told her that when she could get
from her wheelchair into her bed unaided, then she could go home.

Through all these months, Doreen was given the gift of patience
to a degree I had never thought possible. At each setback she would
quietly, but firmly say, 'We'll get there!'

Four and a half years on and Doreen is successfully living in a
flat, driving her car and can take a few steps on her own. In time,
she may be able to walk again. Just because miracles today are
seldom the 'instant' variety, nevertheless, we must never lose sight
of God's healing touch. Whatever our circumstances, our walk with
God is always a journey towards healing and wholeness.

Pray today for the people you know who struggle with ill health.

ER

Journey to faith

... compelled by the Spirit, I am going to Jerusalem, not knowing what will happen to me there...

If Abram was the great man of faith, then the apostle Paul was the great journeyman. By boat and on foot, Paul took the message of the crucified and resurrected Jesus Christ from Jerusalem to Rome.

The miracles of modern travel enable us to travel the world within hours with relative ease and comfort, but spare a thought for the likes of Luke, Barnabas, Mark, Timothy and Paul. We make our journeys with destination and accommodation sorted, but those men were never sure what hostilities they would meet or where indeed they would be able to stay. The things that are for us priorities were incidental in their eyes. Paul especially was driven with evangelistic zeal to share his mind-blowing experience of the risen Christ and, for him, this truth was the transforming power to nurture the greatest gifts within human hearts, namely faith, hope and love.

When I sit on a cliff-top and scribble postcards to friends, it is sometimes difficult to string a few sentences together; trite comments on the weather are mentioned rather than the delight of watching a butterfly or beachcombing. I cannot imagine Paul ever being at a loss for words! His heart and intellect were bursting with this saving knowledge of Christ's sacrifice. He admitted his journey held many dangers, he was ill, stoned, taken in chains, imprisoned and shipwrecked, but he never wavered. What a spiritual explorer!

In a perverse way, we tend to take more notice of a journey peppered with white-knuckle moments and disappointments, rather than a longer adventure completed comfortably. The Acts of the Apostles is a gripping account, not just of physical journeys, but also of the men and women along the way who made their personal journeys to faith in Jesus Christ, the Son of God.

Lord, I pray for those around me who make journeys today, be they physical or spiritual. May each journey be made in faith and hope, surrounded by your eternal love.

ER

The tender call of God

I will lead her into the desert and speak tenderly to her.

This verse was the starting point for me as I stepped into a new dimension of listening to God through the experience of contemplative prayer. It was rather like Lucy's experience in C.S. Lewis' book, *The Lion, the Witch and the Wardrobe*, when she stepped into the wardrobe and entered the land of Narnia.

In Hosea we read of God's enduring love for Israel in the graphic terms of Hosea's love for his unfaithful wife, Gomer. At this poignant moment in the story, we read of an encounter in the desert, impregnated with an undeserved tenderness.

As God leads us into a quiet place in the next few days, whether at home or away on holiday, let us listen to his words to us.

It was not that Gomer, or Israel, deserved this forgiving, tender love of Hosea, or God; in fact, it was the very opposite. The initiative came from God, from his great heart of love and mercy. He, it would seem, is longing for us to hear his invitation to 'Come with me by yourselves into a quiet place and get some rest' (Mark 6:31). We do not, in any way, earn the right to the invitation, nor do we deserve it, but we can delight him by our ready response.

It was this same amazing invitation that first caught my attention when on a clergy wives' retreat several years ago. It wasn't a gilt-edged invitation card that I was given, but it was as clear as that, and very personal. I didn't hear a voice, but it was as if I had a telephone call on a very clear line and someone was waiting for the answer. I had no doubt who that person was.

Breathe on me, breath of God
Fill me with life anew
That I may love what Thou dost love
And do what Thou wouldst do.
EDWIN HATCH (1835–89)

CC

The awesome presence of God

When the Lord saw that he [Moses] had gone over to look, God called to him from within the bush, 'Moses! Moses!'

Moses was alert enough in his spirit to see the bush that was burning but that was not consumed. His response was to go and see whatever was happening and to try to understand the reason for this strange occurrence, but what happened next was not in his calculation! He heard and recognized the voice of God, addressed to him personally. He responded as directed with humble obedience and took off his sandals, understanding that he was standing in the awesome presence of God.

This was surely the key to God speaking again and the beginning of a conversation that would enable his great purposes to be revealed and eventually to be accomplished. It seems that the movement of our spirit that takes us from reading, or even studying, the word of God, to listening to his voice as we read, is rather similar. There is no doubt that reading and studying are vital as we journey through our Christian life. However, it is important also to listen to God speaking to us quite personally; he may have some surprises for us, as he did for Moses. I am continually amazed that the most familiar passages that I have read over many years spring to life in surprising new ways.

I am reminded of the brilliantly coloured fish that I had the privilege of seeing at Eilat in the very south of Israel. It is one thing to see them in the aquarium and to learn their names, even in Latin! It is quite another to swim among them with a snorkel: an unforgettable, vivid experience.

The dimension of your glory, Lord, is something more than we can see in normal ways. It is the colours of the soul that cannot be described with words or paints. In your mercy and your love, we glimpse what we will see in full one day.

CC

Our response—a listening ear

The Lord came and stood there, calling as at other times,
'Samuel! Samuel!' Then Samuel said, 'Speak,
for your servant is listening.'

It is so special to see the ways of God that never change through decades of history as we turn the pages of our Bibles. Yesterday we read of Moses at the burning bush, hearing God's voice addressing him personally, 'Moses, Moses'. Today we read of the same voice calling 'Samuel, Samuel', and this is 300 years or so later. Then there was 'Adam' in the garden of Eden and 'Mary' at the tomb and 'John' on the island of Patmos, it is surely God's way.

Once Samuel realized that it was the Lord speaking, his response was exemplary. He demonstrates unquestioning confidence that the Lord would speak further and that he, Samuel, would not miss a word. Imagine, for a moment, a sheepdog giving his undivided attention to the shepherd. He never takes his eyes off his master's face until the next instruction is given. His body is all aquiver and his ears constantly pricked to catch the slightest hand movement, whistle or word. I imagine that it was like this for Samuel when he responded, 'Speak, Lord, for your servant is listening.'

Let us be very honest now, is this how we come to the living word of God; to our God who has spoken through the ages to his children, if they are truly listening expectantly to him? In every case that we have just thought of in the past few moments there has been an immediate response with huge consequences. Adam came out of hiding; Moses took on the task of leading the people out of Egypt; Samuel began to be obedient to the task of a prophet; Mary sped off at the Lord's bidding to tell the disciples the amazing news of the resurrection, and John turned and received a revelation of the ascended Lord.

Speak, Lord, for your servant is listening.

CC

The grace of radical openness

'I am the Lord's servant,' Mary answered,
'May it be to me as you have said.'

The incarnation depended on Mary being totally open to the work of the Holy Spirit within her; of being receptive to the grace of radical openness, which is a gift from God. The temptations of fear and of needing to understand had to be replaced by total trust in him, and availability to do his will.

On occasions, our primary task is to listen to God as he graciously speaks to us through his living word. At such times, it is not for us to organize what he is going to say, nor to understand fully the meaning of each word, but rather to open the door to his revelation. Mary's question of 'How will this be?' was answered by the assurance of the Holy Spirit's overshadowing, and to this she responded in total trust.

In Revelation 3:20 we are encouraged to respond to God's voice by opening the door. The conversation that ensues is a two-way encounter. Remember the disciples at Emmaus (Luke 24:13–35), when Jesus broke bread with them? They were radically open to what would happen, and had an amazing encounter with the risen Lord. Later that evening they said, 'Were not our hearts burning within us while he talked with us on the road and opened the scriptures to us?'

If we do not limit him to our own concepts, we will find that God is truly a God of surprises! If we can receive the grace of radical openness for all that he has prepared for us through his word, then rest assured we are in for a right royal banquet!

I feel time has stood still for me, this hour of prayer.
A sense of being suspended in the centre of your will.
No longer mine to plan, regret or hurry on…
Just stand, or sit or kneel, and be quite still.
May this become my strong desire,
to be beside as you unfurl your master plan.

CC

Jesus' affirmation of listening

*Mary has chosen what is better, and it will not be
taken away from her.*

As we picture the scene in the home in Bethany of Lazarus and his
sisters, Martha and Mary, we learn some important things about the
heart of God. It is through this cameo, painted for us by Luke, that
Jesus reveals a surprising facet of his Father's love and longing
towards his children. It is surprising because it is not what we are
expecting; not at all how most of us would react to the situation.

Here are two sisters with the unexpected visit of their good
friends, Jesus and his disciples. Martha was the one, it appears, who
opened the door and invited them in. Then immediately she goes to
prepare a meal for the visitors, which would be a normal act of hospitality. But where is Mary? Despite the increasing clatter of prepa-
rations, Mary is sitting at Jesus' feet, listening to his every word. In
the end, Martha can cope no longer. She bursts into the room seeking Jesus' support for her activity on his behalf.

Now here is the surprise! Jesus is clearly delighted with Mary's
choice of activity—her longing to be near and listening to him is
what gives him the greatest joy. It is so important that we take this
in, because it helps us to see this incident from a heavenly perspective. No longer are we focusing on whether Martha was right or
Mary, but seeing the far more important truth, that Jesus wanted the
sisters to be close to him.

This is a tremendous encouragement to us to balance the endless
activity of our Christian lives with unhurried times of listening to
the voice of God through his word. This is in no way a wasted time
or a hobby for some of contemplative nature. This is what our heavenly Father longs for us to do.

---

*Thank you, Lord, for this revelation of your heart's longing. Help me
to spend time in your presence. Let me hear your voice.*

CC

Encouragement to contemplate

Jesus answered, 'Don't you know me, Philip,
even after I have been among you such a long time?
Anyone who has seen me has seen the Father.'

Philip was one of the twelve disciples from the very beginning of Jesus' ministry. We see earlier in John's Gospel, he was one of the first that Jesus called to follow him (John 1:43). Certainly on this occasion towards the end of his life, Jesus refers to his relationship with Philip in terms of 'such a long time'.

When I have led retreats both here in UK and when we lived in Israel, the one question that perhaps I was most frequently asked was 'What exactly is contemplative prayer?' I believe there is confusion about the difference between meditation and contemplation. Meditation is practised in many religious traditions and is often centred on objects of devotion other than Christ, even on inner quiet. Contemplation, however, is to contemplate or look at Christ through the scriptures, in order to understand more about the Trinity— Father, Son and Holy Spirit.

Jesus' words to Philip are the greatest encouragement, and reason, to include a contemplative prayer strand in our spirituality. It is a most profound shift of emphasis for many Christians to let go of an hour or so of activity, however excellent that activity may be, and to contemplate Christ through the scriptures. This is not primarily for guidance or direction, but rather to give a window of time in our hectic lives for God to meet with us and reveal more of himself to us.

I have discovered that very often during such a period of prayer, the Lord shows me something very new about himself. It is almost as if he was waiting for my full attention, in order to reveal heavenly mysteries that expand my vision of him.

O Sabbath rest by Galilee
O calm of hills above,
Where Jesus knelt to share with thee
The silence of eternity
Interpreted by love!
J.G. WHITTIER (1807–92)

CC

Dwelling in his presence

From the ends of the earth I call to you... lead me to the rock that is higher than I... I long to dwell in your tent for ever and take refuge in the shelter of your wings.

The psalmist, probably David, is here concerned with the overriding importance of having a close relationship with God; the sort of one-to-one experience that Moses had when he went into the Tent of Meeting (precursor of the tabernacle). 'There the Lord would speak with Moses face to face, as a man speaks with his friend' (Exodus 33:11). For Moses it was not a 'for ever' experience, because we read of returning to the camp, but it was the vital encounter that he needed as he led the Israelites on through the wilderness.

Remember, too, the occasion on the Mount of Transfiguration when Peter, James, and John had that amazing face-to-face encounter and heard the voice of God, but it was not for ever: 'The next day, when they came down from the mountain...' (Luke 9:37)

There seems to be no doubt at all that the longing of God's heart is that we spend time with him, and that he longs to speak with us, but perhaps the more difficult question to answer is 'for how long, Lord?' For most of us it is impractical to spend whole nights in prayer on a frequent basis, although Jesus did just that on occasion (Luke 6:12). The guideline must surely be the length of time for which we can give maximum, quality concentration to the Lord. We are all different, but that question if honestly answered, may guide us to the period of contemplative prayer that we should begin with. The frequency of such times is another matter to give thought to and, again, for each of us there will be a different answer.

Contemplative prayer is not difficult, but it is a discipline.

Make a prayerful and practical decision (possibly in writing) to his call to you, to come apart by yourself to a quiet place.

CC

Be prepared for the unexpected!

I turned round to see the voice that was speaking to me. And when I turned I saw seven golden lampstands, and among the lampstands was someone 'like a son of man', dressed in a robe reaching down to his feet and with a golden sash round his chest... His face was like the sun shining in all its brilliance.

I can never read this passage in Revelation without a vivid memory of an afternoon in Tel Aviv. I was leading a small group through a course entitled 'Venture into Contemplative Prayer'. They had gone off to a quiet place on their own with this passage of scripture for half an hour and were returning to our bungalow to share their experiences.

Through the door came the one with the greatest question marks about the venture. Her face was radiant, almost glowing. She could not wait for 'her turn', but burst out with the fact that she had done just as the apostle John had done; she had stood and turned and met the ascended Lord, face to face. None of us in the room could doubt the reality of her encounter.

Perhaps yesterday you made a serious response to build into your prayer life times of quiet, contemplative, listening prayer. If so, then be prepared for some surprises of great joy that will be of great inner strengthening to your spirit. Already in the past week of readings, we have seen, from Genesis to Revelation, that he is truly a God of surprises. Think of Adam, Moses, young Samuel, Hosea, Mary at the annunciation, the disciples on the mountain, Mary at the tomb and the disciples on the road to Emmaus, to name but a few; and remember that our God never changes: 'But now, God's Message... "Don't be afraid, I've redeemed you. I've called your name. You're mine..."' (Isaiah 43:1, THE MESSAGE).

How silently, how silently,
The wondrous gift is given!
So God imparts to human hearts
The blessings of his heaven.

PHILIP BROOKS (1835–93)

CC

Moses' face was radiant

When Moses came down from Mount Sinai with the two tablets of the Testimony in his hands, he was not aware that his face was radiant because he had spoken with the Lord.

Through the Old and New Testament passages of the past eight days, we have been seeing the Lord's longing to speak with his children. We have seen also the importance of being alert to his voice and being prepared to stop and listen to him. Now for the next six days we will have the opportunity to do just that and to contemplate the shining glory of his presence. It would be best, if at all possible, to read the full passage for each day and not just the verse that is printed out.

The notes will guide your contemplation, but only that. The primary aim will be to encourage your personal listening. This will lead to an encounter that will be different for each person. I suggest that you take time to be quiet before you begin, possibly playing some quiet music or lighting a candle, or both!

This is all going to take too long, you may be thinking, but if we are seeking to meet with our heavenly Father, we should be prepared for that. August holidays may give you the space you need. Moses was prepared to climb Mount Sinai in order for a close encounter to take place. (That is no easy task I can tell you from personal experience, even with the help of a camel for some of the way!)

Read the account slowly and let the words become more than words: the voice of God speaking to you and enabling you to share in Moses' experience. What arrests your attention most: the radiance of Moses' face; his total lack of awareness of this; the fact that he had spoken with the Lord; his longing to share his experience, or something quite new and surprising—a word that you feel can only be from him?

Write down this 'word' or thought.

CC

111

Isaiah 6:1–8 (NIV)

Isaiah's vision

Holy, holy, holy is the Lord Almighty;
the whole earth is full of his glory.

Today we move approximately seven centuries on in the history of Israel to another close encounter with the Lord Almighty, this time with the prophet Isaiah. This encounter has many parallels with Moses on Mount Sinai where we were yesterday. When Isaiah saw the Lord, high and exalted and surrounded by heavenly beings he, like Moses at the burning bush and on Mount Sinai, was aware of his unworthiness. Isaiah was especially aware of his unclean lips.

The clouds and the smoke and the covering of faces all tell us of the infinite holiness of God; the glory is there as well. It is this same glory that lights up our eyes, surely, when we see a summer sunset reflected in the sea. The whole earth is truly full of his glory and we can echo the well-known words of Elizabeth Barrett Browning: 'Earth's crammed with heaven / And every common bush afire with God. / But only he who sees, takes off his shoes.'

To contemplate the Lord leads us also to a heightened awareness of our own shortcomings and of the need to repent. It is not possible to rush into his presence without first asking for his cleansing and forgiveness. He has not changed and we can be confident of his response to our confession and ensuing close encounter. The cleansing comes from him, the confession and repentance is from us. Remember, 'If we confess our sins, he is faithful and just and will forgive us our sins' (1 John 1:9).

Let us now come into his presence with a quiet heart and contemplate him through the vision of Isaiah. What aspect of this vision speaks most loudly to you? Be open to his revelation of himself and then record today's focal point for you.

It is a thing most wonderful,
Almost too wonderful to be,
That God's own son should come from heaven,
And die to save a child like me.

W. WALSHAM HOW (1823–97)

CC

Transfiguration

As he was praying, the appearance of his face changed, and his clothes became as bright as a flash of lightning.

Now we have moved on again to the New Testament, so things are bound to be different—or are they? When we know that God remains the same (Psalm 102:27) and 'Jesus Christ is the same yesterday, today and for ever' (Hebrews 13:8), then it is not surprising to see the shining glory of his presence spanning the scriptures from beginning to end.

Travel up Mount Hermon with Jesus and the three disciples and picture the scene as it unfolds before your eyes. Feel the stones beneath your feet and the diminishing sounds of the villages you have left behind you. Contemplate Jesus as he stops to pray and catch the wonder of his transfiguration. Things are happening that are beyond human experience and dimensions of colour that can only be described as heavenly; not to mention the appearance of Moses and Elijah talking with him. Moments like these can only be responded to with awe and wonder. It is as if a corner of the heavens has been peeled back and we are responding with stillness.

Peter's response is very human and understandable: 'Let's put up three shelters…' Today we might say, 'Let's make a video of this!' In other words, we are tempted at such moments to earth our glimpse of heaven, but that is not the way. Rather, be still and allow yourself to be led further, into the cloud (reminiscent of Moses and Isaiah), and hear the voice of the Lord our God revealing more as he chooses.

When the moments of encounter pass, as they surely will, we must be prepared to let go. Such precious times are not always for sharing, but for doing as Mary did soon after Jesus' birth (Luke 2:19 and 51). Rest assured, such real encounters will not fade.

Fading is the worldling's pleasure
All his boasted pomp and show;
Solid joys and lasting treasure
None but Zion's children know.
JOHN NEWTON (1725–1807)

CC

Stephen's vision

But Stephen, full of the Holy Spirit, looked up to heaven and saw the glory of God, and Jesus standing at the right hand of God.

We are moving on again, today, to the time soon after Jesus' ascension to his Father in heaven. We know that Stephen had recently been chosen to help the disciples in the administration of food for both Hebrew and Greek widows, in the fast-growing fellowship of believers in Jerusalem (Acts 6:1–8). He was a man who was full of faith and of the Holy Spirit and God's power and wisdom. He was also singled out by the Jewish authorities to be made an example of, as their power was once again under threat.

It is clear, therefore, that as we contemplate passages of scripture, it is very important to be aware of the context in which they occur. It is only then that we are able to appreciate accurately and fully the riches of the words that we are 'listening to'.

Let us return now to our passage for today and the vision of Stephen in the midst of a furious mob. It was hardly a moment of peace and quiet music, and I am sure there was not a candle in sight! It was, rather, his availability to the Spirit of God and the fact that he was looking up to heaven that enabled him to see the glory of God and the ascended Jesus standing at God's right hand.

I am sure there are no achievement awards attached to drawing close to the throne room of heaven, but, rather, an openness of heart and spirit for God's in-filling as we look towards him. There is no doubt that as you contemplate Stephen's vision and are in that open frame of mind and heart, you can expect a close encounter of God's choosing, so be prepared!

Contemplate Stephen's vision, and then record your special word or thought for today or the verse that you spent longest with.

CC

The ascended Lord

I turned round to see the voice that was speaking to me...
[He] said: 'Do not be afraid...'

When we read passages like this, it is tempting to feel somewhat envious of John who seems to have experienced a spiritual *son et lumière*, such as we have never experienced. However, on closer reading it is clear that John was not on a luxury retreat on the island of Patmos, but, rather, in exile and possible isolation not of his choosing. It was on the Lord's Day. He was turning his thoughts to the things of the Spirit, in discipline and obedience, when he had a powerful encounter with the Lord. He responded without question or doubt.

How often, when we are in a difficult season in our life, do we continue with the disciplined practice of setting time aside to draw near to God, in spite of the circumstance that we are experiencing? It might be that you are in just such a situation. May I encourage you to do just what John did on the island of Patmos—turn your spirit towards the Lord, whatever you are feeling, and trust him to come to you. It may not be immediately or dramatically, but certainly, by the end of the day, I believe, you will have knowledge of his presence that is not of your making.

It is good to read of John's simple action of 'turning' in response to the sound of the voice of God. Then, as a consequence of his obedience and lack of questioning, he had this amazing vision of the ascended Lord Jesus. Sometimes for us, too, it is a simple act of obedience that leads us on to a deeper experience of him, such as we thought only happened to others. Do you remember how Jesus encouraged Simon to push out into the deeper water and, to his great surprise, they caught such a large number of fish that their nets began to break? (Luke 5:4–6)

Try 'pushing out' on your special word today.

CC

A review of his speaking

*... these are written that you may believe that Jesus is
the Christ, the Son of God, and that by believing
you may have life in his name.*

I wonder how John selected the material that he included in his
Gospel, have you ever thought of that? It must have been a process
of reviewing all the wonderful things that Jesus said and did during
the three years of his life with John and the other disciples and seeing the main strands that emerged. Those things that would best
communicate his divinity: the Word that 'became flesh and made
his dwelling among us' (John 1:14).

At the end of these days of contemplation, it would be good for
us to review the main strands that have emerged as we have listened
and contemplated. If you did record your special words, it would be
good to re-read them prayerfully now and see the colours of the jew-
els that you have received and the pattern that they create in you.
If we do not record God's words to us, it gives Satan a chance to
snatch them away, and it must sadden the heart of God to see how
little we value his speaking to us.

So often, we see that he instructs his prophets to 'Go now, write
it on a tablet for them, inscribe it on a scroll' (Isaiah 30:8). No easy
task in the days of yesteryear. We have ballpoint pens spilling out of
every corner, not to mention paper, but are too lazy to record the
precious words that God speaks, when we listen.

A review period of prayer is like a costly Persian rug, with its rich
colours of purple and red. How sad it would be if the weavers of the
rug had failed to knot off the ends with a fringe, so the pattern and
'story' of the colours soon unravelled and were lost.

---

*Let us record the colours and patterns of these days of contemplation
and determine to go on with our life of listening prayer.*

CC

116

Ephesians 1:3–14 (NRSV)

Blessing God for blessing us

Blessed be the God and Father of our Lord Jesus Christ,
who has blessed us in Christ with every spiritual blessing
in the heavenly places.

Paul begins this letter with praise for all the blessings Christians
have in Christ. In the original Greek, all 11 verses are one sentence.
To get the feel of the passage it helps to read it aloud very fast!
Because it's not easy to divide into neat portions, the whole passage
will be set for each day's reading this week. Try using different Bible
versions to make the most of these amazing verses.

What makes you pray? How do you begin? I have to admit that,
more often than not, it is problems and difficulties that push me to
pray. If I were in prison, alone, having travelled hundreds of miles
on foot, sometimes very hungry, thrown out of villages, beaten up,
like Paul, I would not find it easy to begin with praise. Paul, though,
writing to small groups of Christian believers, some of them slaves
and many certainly poor, doesn't begin with the hard things. He
begins with praise, not just praise because God is God, but grateful
passionate praise for all God has done for him and for all Christians.
It is a wonderful outpouring of blessing upon blessing.

Absorbed with work, home, money, weather, relationships and
shopping, maybe we do sometimes ask ourselves what difference
being a Christian makes. Heads down, we see only that everything
is grey; but lift up your eyes, says Paul, and look at the glory of the
sun. We have probably heard passages like this before, but so often,
too often, we live as if they were not really true. Lift up your eyes,
look up, realize the blessings upon blessings you have in Christ and
praise him for them.

Read the passage again. Count the number of times the phrase 'in
Christ', or 'in him', comes. Are you 'in Christ'—a new creation?
Then praise him that nothing can separate us from him and all these
blessings.

MK

The blessing of a fresh start

Because of the sacrifice of the Messiah, his blood poured out on the altar of the Cross, we're a free people—free of penalties and punishments chalked up by all our misdeeds.

Paul uses the word 'we' as he describes the blessings that God gives to all Christians, but in verse 13 he changes to 'you'. 'It's in Christ that you, once you heard the truth and believed it [this message of your salvation], found yourselves home free—signed, sealed, and delivered by the Holy Spirit.'

Once his readers had been outside the blessing of God, but when they heard the word of truth they knew they needed a fresh start and forgiveness so, turning to Jesus, they became Christians.

How do we live with the things we cannot bear anyone to know about? How do we bear the burden of cruel words we cannot withdraw? What do we do with a past we cannot change? There is a way, through Jesus' blood shed on the cross, Paul says.

When we hear the word of truth and respond, knowing we need forgiveness and salvation, then the Father's arms are open for us, and all these blessings in Christ are ours—the blessing of forgiveness and peace, the past put behind us and a fresh start. The riches of God's grace are there to be lavished on us—freely given, however bad, however destructive we have been. There are costs to this blessing, though. First, there is the cost that Jesus paid, for all these blessings come through his sacrifice. Then there is also a cost for us; admitting what we have done and seeking forgiveness.

There is also a cost in dealing with the hurts we receive from others. We pray 'Forgive us our sins as we forgive those who sin against us'. Overwhelmed by his loving forgiveness, our response is to begin the process of forgiving others.

Forgive us our sins, Lord, and help us to forgive others, freely and ungrudgingly so that they too may know the riches of your grace.
MK

The blessing of being chosen

Long ago, even before he made the world, God loved us and chose us in Christ to be holy and without fault in his eyes.

The world is a big place full of six billion people. How can I have been chosen before the creation of the world? Jesus understood how difficult it is to grasp God's particular care for each of us. He said, 'Not even a sparrow, worth only half a penny, can fall to the ground without your Father knowing it. And the very hairs on your head are all numbered. So don't be afraid; you are more valuable to him than a whole flock of sparrows' (Matthew 10:29–31). Paul doesn't just talk about God's particular care for his children each day, however. He adds that we were chosen before the world began, named and special before creation.

Sometimes it is hard to accept that we are chosen and special to God. Failed interviews, being left out of school teams, failed relationships, can colour our estimation of ourselves. Becoming a Christian and beginning the journey of faith is the beginning of healing. Slowly the Holy Spirit works that chosenness and love into the deep and secret places of low self-worth. We as individuals today, whatever our past and whatever our present, are beloved, chosen before the foundation of the world, fully known.

There is another side to this. These wonderful blessings of ours are not to be hugged to ourselves in delight. If we are forgiven and chosen, then so are our fellow Christians, and these gifts of grace are on offer for anyone who comes to him. We do not know who is chosen, so we should treat people as if they all are. We have to accept a divine valuation, not a human one.

Rejoice in being chosen by God. Then ask yourself if there is anyone you need to reassess as a chosen one and, by your love, begin their restoration to the fullness of blessing as a child of God.

MK

The blessing of being adopted

He destined us for adoption as his children through Jesus Christ according to the good pleasure of his will.

Those who have spent part of their young lives in children's homes understand the longing to be adopted, to be chosen and made part of a family, legally, for ever. But they have to wait, sometimes for a very long time, to know the love and care of parents. (The shortage of foster and adoptive parents should be a concern for all Christians and should encourage us to see this as a possible calling.)

When it comes to our relationship with our heavenly Father, he is the one who waits to adopt *us*, for we can be reluctant, obstinate and disobedient—unwilling to go home to him.

Jesus told the story of three losses: a sheep, a coin and a son. Both the sheep and coin, which couldn't help being lost, were searched for, found and taken home; but the son had deliberately left home and his father had to wait until he made that return journey in repentance and humility. Then, instead of being given a lowly place as a servant for wasting his inheritance, he was forgiven, welcomed, dressed in the finest clothes and a party was held in his honour.

Many leave home without a backward glance, as soon as they can, only realizing later the value of love, stability, roots and acceptance that family life at its best gives us as we grow into adulthood. In the same way, we can lose sight of our rich blessings as adopted heirs of our Father, as brothers and sisters of Christ, welcomed into the family of faith.

Someone I knew adopted five children from very different backgrounds. In our Christian fellowships we are like that family. Chosen by a heavenly Father to be adopted as brothers and sisters, heirs to all his riches, secure for ever.

Look round next time you are with your fellow Christians and thank the Lord that you and they are all adopted by him.

MK

The blessing of a glorious future

*He destined us for adoption as his children through Jesus Christ,
according to the good pleasure of his will... he has made known to
us the mystery of his will... that he set forth in Christ, as a plan
for the fullness of time, to gather up all things in him.*

Paul's words fall over themselves as he pours out his praise. Every
spiritual blessing is lavished on us freely, and it is all according to
God's pleasure—a hymn of praise to the overwhelming generosity of
God to us in this world—and in the heavenly realms. There is no
place in heaven or earth that the overflowing glory of God does not
reach. In one sense we already have all these blessings now, but we
will not experience them fully until we receive our inheritance, at
the final party and banquet in heaven.

   This is a vision of such splendour and richness that it should
colour every moment of our lives. Moreover, if we are in Christ, we
have the best seats in the house to see the grand finale of the whole
of time. If you know which general is going to win the war, then it
is wise to stick with him. However tough it gets in the meantime, we
are guaranteed to be there when his glory is revealed and everyone
who has ever lived will see him on the throne of heaven as Saviour,
Judge and King.

Finish then thy new creation:
Pure and spotless let us be;
Let us see thy great salvation,
Perfectly restored in thee:
Changed from glory into glory,
Till in heaven we take our place,
Till we cast our crowns before thee,
Lost in wonder love and praise.

CHARLES WESLEY (1707–88)

MK

The blessing of purpose

For he chose us in him before the creation of the world to be holy and blameless in his sight.

It is hard not to have some kind of purpose for each day. Even having hard things to do, a job that is stressful or the care of someone demanding, can provide structure and satisfaction. We may long for a demanding situation to end, but when it does we may feel bereft, without focus or aim.

It is even harder to have no sense of purpose for life, to feel that nothing is worthwhile, but many people do feel like that. So it really is a blessing to be chosen by God for the purpose of being holy and blameless. It may seem too vague, or even too hard, but it is a blessing that involves adventure and challenge and enormous satisfaction.

It means that everything we do, say and think, we seek to do God's way, obeying his commands, imitating his character and growing all the fruit of the Spirit—and that takes a lifetime. So we may still have a hard and tiring job, we may still be caring for someone who is difficult, but there is a way of doing those tasks that brings glory to God and makes us more holy.

How do we do this? We need to learn how to pray. We need to read the Bible, so that we know it so well that it shapes our thinking. We need to learn and pray with others, so that we help each other grow in holiness. We need to understand the world around us, so that we can recognize unholiness when we see it. We need to work to make the world more like his kingdom of love, justice and peace.

We also know that, although we will never be perfectly holy and blameless in this life, when we stand before him on the final great day, then the fullness of this blessing will be ours.

Read Revelation 7:9–17 as a reminder of what is in store.

MK

The blessing of fellowship

And you also were included in Christ... Having believed, you were marked in him with a seal, the promised Holy Spirit, who is a deposit guaranteeing our inheritance... to the praise of his glory.

We have a big problem when New Testament Greek is translated into modern English. Because we use 'you' for the singular and the plural, we can read whole chunks of Paul's letters and hear him speaking to us as individual Christians rather than to Christian fellowships as a whole.

The message of the whole Bible is that we follow the Lord together. We cannot, nor are we expected to function as Christians on our own. All the pictures of the Church—the people of God, the branches of the vine, the parts of the body, a house built with living stones—show us that we work together in close relationship with those God has called together in a local fellowship.

Together we should be showing what the new kingdom of God looks like in practice. Together we praise and worship him for all his blessings. Together we work out what these blessings mean in our lives, teaching, encouraging, sharing and sometimes admonishing one another—above all, loving and blessing one another as he has loved and blessed us. We go out from that fellowship, renewed and inspired, into our weekday lives of work and home, as the scattered Church of God, carrying in us the inner joy of his lavish blessings, forgiven, chosen, adopted and secure for ever.

Well, of course, it isn't always like that. Even the best fellowships don't get it right all the time, but then they are made up of people learning and growing in Christ as they go. We need to be realistic about ourselves and our churches and sure of all his blessings.

Before moving on, read this passage again, pause and meditate on the blessings we have in Christ and turn them into a prayer of praise.

MK

Feasting with God

… they beheld God, and they ate and drank.

When I stumbled across this verse I did a double take: 'They beheld God and they ate and drank'. The sublime and the mundane embrace! The awesome God and the people of Israel had just made a covenant, a marriage-like agreement, that they would be faithful to each other. The Israelites saw something of the invisible God— and celebrated in a sort of wedding breakfast. Good gracious, if I had just 'seen' God (whatever that means), I think even I would lose my appetite!

Yet eating meals is much more than putting food in our mouths. Eating involves not only teeth and tongue and stomach, but also heart and head and soul. When we eat together, we are saying: 'I am needy! I am human! I am vulnerable! I am sharing my food, my life, my frailty, my feelings with you.' A meal seals and strengthens relationships. God is with us as we become family, friends and community.

If your relationship with God is a meal, how would you describe it? Is it eaten from bone china, special and romantic but polite and unreal? Is it in chipped crockery, part of everyday life, but routine and dull? Is it a fondue, always a group activity and never personal? Does it come in a paper bag as fast food, a hurried, nodding acquaintance with minimal nourishment? Perhaps it is taken with chopsticks, having promise of the exotic but the sense that you will never master it. Or is it best described as an infant's meal, childlike but also childish, or a picnic, fun, but only when it is not raining?

God can be in all these 'less than ideal' meals, and more. The wonderful promise is that when we pledge ourselves to him, he comes into every part of our lives, even our eating and drinking.

'I will come in to you and eat with you, and you with me' (Revelation 3:20b). *Invite him in today!*

FB

Angels unawares

Do not neglect to show hospitality to strangers, for by doing that some have entertained angels without knowing it

'Don't talk to strangers', we rightly tell children, and then follow our own advice. With good reason. The news tells of unscrupulous characters out to plunder our lives and rob us of our peace of mind. We pull up the drawbridge on our homes, huddle in cliques for safety and mix with people who are 'our types'.

We could be shutting out angels. We are also excluding the lonely, the hungry, the stranger: those whom Jesus loves and accepts.

Abraham lived in dangerous days, too. Far from the security of his home town, he was at the mercy of robbers and harsh natural conditions. He understood the perils of lonely travel, so he actually reached out to strangers rather than recoiling from them.

When Abraham spotted three men passing by his tent, he ran to offer them water, rest and a wash. The story is told in Genesis 18:1–8. 'Let me bring you a little bread,' he added to his welcome, and proceeded to lavish meat, milk and cakes on them.

What if he had closed his eyes to those strangers? He would have missed a visit from the Lord himself. What if he had cautioned himself not take risks? He would never have heard that promise, his deepest desire: 'Sarah shall have a son' (v. 14).

Living in a university town, I meet many who have travelled with their families to study and work. Some are Christians, but most are Buddhists or atheists, Muslims or Hindus. Far from home and eager to meet new people, they can encounter suspicion or even hostility. As they valiantly chew through my lentil stews and other culinary disasters, these strangers become friends. My horizons expand, my cultural understanding deepens and my list of holiday destinations grows! I have indeed entertained angels. Christ has visited me.

'I was hungry and you gave me food… I was a stranger and you welcomed me' (Matthew 25:35). What 'strangers' could you invite?

FB

Family meals

*... when your children ask you, 'What do you mean
by this observance?' you shall say, 'It is the passover
sacrifice to the Lord'.*

The other night, a TV programme on fast food showed a scene
enacted in thousands of homes across the UK: a busy mum trying to
cater for different tastes. As various ready meals waited in a queue
to be microwaved, we watched her standing in front of the television eating her own. Meanwhile, her husband was in the kitchen
sawing through his three burnt sausages and blackened chips.

While my sympathies are with the harassed mother, I couldn't
help thinking that this family is missing out on more than nutrition.
The television and sofa have replaced dining table and chairs. Soap
characters are probably closer than the 'strangers' to whom they are
related and with whom they live.

What a contrast to the opportunities presented by the Passover,
one of several significant feasts in the Jewish calendar! This family
meal, instituted as the Jewish people were rushing to escape from
Egypt, has been celebrated in millions of homes throughout history.
Year after year, the food itself tells the story of national slavery and
of God's deliverance: bitter herbs recall bitter suffering; the unleav-
ened bread demonstrates the haste with which the fleeing people
cooked and ate; the lamb reminds everyone of the animal killed in
place of the eldest son. The meal has kindled a sense of identity for
a community and for individuals within it.

Family meals are wonderful occasions in which to face each other
and tell our stories. We share not only food, but time and the stuff
that makes up our days. We talk about mundane affairs and repeat
experiences and memories across the generations. In conversation, we discover who we are and from where we have come. As
Christians, our stories inevitably include God's hand in our lives. He
is the one who gives meaning and direction and hope to our future
as we journey together.

How might my family meals be better used for storytelling?

FB

Feed the world

*At twilight you shall eat meat, and in the morning
you shall have your fill of bread.*

Where does our food come from? Well, it comes from the kitchen
cupboards. It comes from the supermarket. It comes from somewhere or other in big vans. For those who live removed from farming and the rural way of life, it is easy to forget that our food comes
from God. He is the one who provides.

The Israelites were in a wilderness. Their children were crying.
They were hungry. Suddenly slavery didn't seem so bad after all.
After all, you can't eat freedom—and there didn't seem to be much
else on offer.

God heard their complaints, and sent them quail for tea and
bread (or manna) for breakfast. Manna was a flaky substance left on
the ground by the dew. It tasted like wafers made with honey. God's
instructions were very precise: each day, the people were to gather
only as much as they needed. Any leftovers went bad overnight.
However, the day before the Sabbath, they were to collect enough
for two days and, amazingly, that stayed fresh. So, for 40 years,
morning by morning, young and old were reminded that they were
utterly dependent on God for their sustenance.

Statisticians tell us that 50 per cent of the world today suffers
from malnutrition. How does God answer the prayers of those who,
like the Israelites, cry, 'Give us this day our daily bread'?

Is it through us? Are we gathering more of what God has provided than we should? Are we storing food and hoarding our wealth
because we don't really trust God to give us what we need for each
day? Is our greed leaving others in need? Could we exert more con-
sumer power to ensure that the tea and coffee farmers are fairly
paid? Might we give so that millions, hungry through drought, flood
or war, might share in the bounty that God has lavished on his
world?

---

*Lord, give us this day our daily bread—not too much so we are sick,
but enough to share!*

FB

Leviticus 9:22–24 (NRSV)

Burnt offerings

The glory of the Lord appeared to all the people. Fire came out from the Lord and consumed the burnt-offering and the fat on the altar.

The season of barbecues is upon us—long, light, lazy evenings of chat and charcoal. Friends gather clutching salads and beefburgers. Children run in circles round the garden. Men who never go near a kitchen cooker take possession of the grill in the ultimate macho test. Inevitably, proceedings are interrupted several times by mad dashes to shelter from the rain, and your paper plate bows under the weight of unappealing 'burnt fat'.

Had we lived in Old Testament days, the burning of meat would not have been confined to sociable summers. It was an indispensable part of worship. Israelites brought everyday animal and grain foodstuffs as their offerings to God. The blood shed indicated life lost, an animal serving as substitute for a sinful person. Sacrifices expressed thanksgiving and repentance, petition and promise, dedication and communion.

Afterwards, meat was sometimes shared by priests and worshippers. This feasting was integral to grateful worship because God had provided for their physical needs throughout the year and also for their sins to be forgiven. When the priests began this ministry in Leviticus 9, the fire from God was a sign that he had accepted their sacrifice and they were blessed.

Today we enjoy (or endure!) barbecues for fun, not for forgiveness. What has changed? Jesus is the perfect once-and-for-all sacrifice. He died instead of us so that our relationship with God might be put right. We are blessed beyond words; we are loved beyond clichés; we are forgiven beyond all condemnation; and so we give ourselves back to God as living sacrifices, living day by day as thankful and willing servants and friends.

As you relax over singed sausages and marshmallows, thank God for new life! Thank God for Jesus!

'Take your everyday, ordinary life—your sleeping, eating, going-to-work, and walking around life—and place it before God as an offering' (Romans 12:1, THE MESSAGE)

FB

Abigail's picnic

Abigail... took two hundred loaves, two skins of wine, five sheep... five measures of parched grain, one hundred clusters of raisins, and two hundred cakes of figs.

I find it hard to forgive people who make me suffer, especially when they don't seem to care. Of course, as a good Christian, I don't have any 'enemies' as such, but my wounded feelings often wrestle with God's command that I should love those who hurt me. After prayer, pleading, sulking and anger, I have hit on another course of action: there is nothing that makes your enemies feel worse than when you are nice to them. Give them a meal!

That is what Abigail did. When she had heard that David was on his way to butcher her husband Nabal and his men, she sprang into action. She gathered an enticing picnic and rushed to meet him. Falling on her knees, she reminded David of God's certain calling on his life as future king and pleaded with him to avoid bloodshed.

She knew why David was outraged. Outlawed by King Saul, he had been living with his men in the semi-barren area of Judah. It was difficult to find food. One enterprising way was to offer security and protection to farmers from raiders, in the hope of provisions. David was furious when feast time came at the farm of wealthy Nabal and he was not invited. The rejection, along with all his other worries, made him overreact. No one was going to stop him from venting his fury on this stupid, mean man.

No one, that is, except the clever and beautiful Abigail. I don't know whether it was her intelligence or her looks or her picnic that stopped David in his tracks, but the story ends with Nabal dying of shock when he hears what happened and David marrying Abigail.

Don't underestimate the power of a cheese sandwich! It will disarm your enemy. It may even disarm you.

'If your enemies are hungry, give them bread to eat...' (Psalm 25:21a). Who, Lord?

FB

Fasting and feasting

*… days of feasting and gladness, days for sending gifts of food
to one another and presents to the poor.*

There can be two types of feasting: feasting to forget and feasting to
remember. Feasting to forget often involves lavish entertainment,
where food and drink flow in abundance, and guests exclaim over
presentation, taste and extravagance. That was Xerxes', king of the
Persian empire's, style. Week-long parties for nobles and officials
served to feed his appetite for jollity and manipulation. We are no
strangers to such a need to impress, where the fragile egos of the rich
and famous are greedy for adulation.

The trouble was that all this feasting made him forget reality and
responsibility. He denied respect to his wife, so when the queen
refused to perform in front of his drunken audience, she exposed his
own shaky self-worth. So he would not remember, she was promptly
deposed and another young, compliant beautiful replacement called
Esther was found.

Xerxes forgot that being a king is about fair rule, so when his
deputy Haman suggested the annihilation of the Jewish people
(because one Jew, Esther's cousin, offended him) he agreed to it
without question, more concerned with wine than the fate of God's
people.

The Jewish community responded with desperate fasting and
mourning. After three days of no food or drink, Queen Esther
received guidance and courage to approach the king and invite him
to two banquets. There, amid the eating and drinking, she pleaded
with him for her life and that of her people.

So the story ends with feasting, but now it is feasting to remember. Together, year after year, in the Feast of Purim, the Jews recall
their powerlessness in those dark events. They recollect how the
seemingly absent God had not abandoned them to chance or to a
carousing, forgetful despot. God's thankful people, rich and poor,
celebrate his deliverance as a community and share in the feast.

---

*Are my parties and anniversary meals times of thankful recollection
of God's hand in my community's life—or distractions from them?*

FB

Not cordon bleu

There is a boy here who has five barley loaves and two fish. But what are they among so many people?

Tonight our neighbours are coming for a meal. We are a bit nervous: what are we going to cook? We have had them enough times to have exhausted our meagre repertoire of dishes. I have even resorted to recipe books in search of inspiration, but retreated in fear. Home from an abortive attempt at finding the solution on supermarket shelves, I recall what one of our victims wrote in the visitors' book, 'Better a meal of vegetables where there is love than a fattened calf with hatred' (Proverbs 15:17, NIV). I cling on to that as my hospitality motto and just hope our friends like vegetables baked in love.

So now as I turn from menu despair to the feeding of the 15,000 (15,000 because I include the women and children!), I am enormously heartened. I am especially drawn to the boy who enabled it to happen. We are not told his name or his age. In the four Gospel accounts, only John mentions him. However, what he did has resonated through history.

Barley loaves were poor people's bread, and the fish would probably be a pickled side dish. Yet their quantity and simplicity did not stop him from offering them to Jesus. He had heard that Jesus wanted to feed the hungry. That was enough for him. Throwing selfishness and his own limitations aside, he focused on Jesus, who could do anything. He didn't care what cynics or realists or chefs thought. It didn't matter if it was sensible or not, or if some of the kids he didn't like got fed, too.

In exchange, he saw something wonderful: Jesus' love transformed the simple food he shared. His story reminds this panic-stricken hostess that Jesus can turn ordinary morsels into something deeply satisfying. It is God's blessing on my dubious cooking that rescues the meal. Most importantly, Jesus is honoured when it is served not with pride, but with love.

Thank you, Jesus, for multiplying what I lovingly bring to you— beyond my wildest imaginings.

FB

Jesus' love feast

*... as often as you eat this bread and drink this cup, you proclaim
the Lord's death until he comes.*

Mealtimes can be exhausting. Put a family together around a dining
table and, before the plates are cleared, complaints, tensions and
raised voices can fly around like missiles. Food remains uneaten,
cooks feel unappreciated and everyone retreats to lick their wounds.
'It's not meant to be like that,' thousands of us say to ourselves.
'I bet no one else has such an awful time.'

They do. Eating with others is a vulnerable experience. We share
ourselves as well as our food, and that may be sweet or sour.

It is wonderfully ironic that Jesus chose a meal to help us remember what he has done for us. The torn, lowly bread demonstrates
how his body was broken. The poured-out wine shows how his
blood flowed. Since then, every time his friends take bread and
wine, they remind themselves that their forgiveness has come at the
cost of Jesus' life. It is eloquent beyond language and history.

If only we could eat in splendid pious isolation! It would be much
less messy. Yet feasting with God involves communion with others.
The Corinthians squabbled and the rich had little sensitivity for
their hungry fellow believers. Sadly, over the centuries, Jesus' table
has continued as a place of ugly fighting. Repeatedly we have forgotten that the very taking of the elements is an acknowledgment
that we are all sinners. Only Jesus' death can save us. Only his life
can nourish us and fill our hungry hearts.

Last Sunday I watched as people went forward for communion:
young and old, fat and thin, happy and sad, black and white, native
British, Japanese, German and Korean, my friends and so-called
'enemies'. I was reminded that we all share equally in the one bread
and the one cup, we are all imperfect and we all depend on Jesus—
for better, for worse.

'Every time you eat... Every time you drink, remember me.' Lord,
help me to love your table guests, for your sake!

FB

The perfect dinner party

'How fortunate the one who gets to eat dinner in God's kingdom!'

One day the sausages won't burn and the curry will have just the right amount of spice, the jelly will set properly and the pavlova won't implode. The food will appear effortlessly on the table and everyone will enjoy each dish. The people I love will be beside me and there will be no painful absences. The dinner conversation will be funny, warm and invigorating with no awkward silences or tactless remarks. Most importantly, one day, an entire meal of chocolate will be nourishing and not make me fat. In my dreams…

… and in God's plan (though perhaps some of the details are my own creation). For God has been preparing a heavenly banquet for years. The Lord of all the earth, who has everything at his disposal, is laying on a sumptuous wedding feast to celebrate his love for us. That is why Jesus came: to invite us to eat with him in his home for ever.

Who could refuse? It is free: he paid for our place at the table. There is no trick: we simply have to accept.

Jesus' parable of the great banquet startles us. Told in response to a pious sentiment—'How fortunate the one who gets to eat dinner in God's kingdom!'—Jesus shows that many find short-sighted excuses not to attend. Work, consumerism and family are still factors that make people reject the best offer of their lives.

For those who accept, there is glorious hope. One day all our inner hunger and longings and disappointments will be swallowed up. We will see the great feast-giver face to face. As we gather around the banqueting table, we will embrace people from north, south, east and west. We will be satisfied to the very depths of our beings. As his body, his bride, we will be with our bridegroom for ever.

'Quickly, get out into the city streets and alleys. Collect all who look like they need a square meal… I want my house full!' Who can you invite?

FB

DAY
BY
DAY
WITH
GOD

MAGAZINE SECTION

What the Bible means to me

Margaret Mankey

I was diagnosed with schizophrenia thirty years ago. I was in a mental hospital, interviewed and observed by overworked psychiatrists and psychiatric nurses; judged, misunderstood, jeered at for praying but loved by other patients. It was a long-stay hospital and permanent home to many. I enlisted some help and moved the furniture around in the sitting-room of the Women's Admission Ward, hunted for wood and coal, and lit a fire in the grate each day in winter. I organized serving tea to patients' visitors, which was stopped when the staff did an inventory and couldn't account for hundreds of teabags and pounds of biscuits!

I was so emotionally tired that I knew I was not making sense or getting through to my questioners, but later, in my desolation, I picked up the Gideon Bible at my hospital bedside and re-read the Psalms and Gospels. I quickly learned that the Bible understood me, and, praise God, I understood the Bible. It wasn't just a few verses that leaped out of the page—all its truths and descriptions made sense and became relevant to understanding biblical characters, situations, myself, other people and, above all, God.

When we pass through times of sickness, suffering and tribulation, we should remember that Christ is in it with us. The Bible seems to say, also, that it is health-giving for us to examine our actions and attitudes; to recognize where we have sinned and to ask forgiveness; to recognize where we have been sinned against and to ask for grace to forgive; to recognize where circumstances were and are beyond our control and the result of living in a fallen world, and ask for grace to accept, endure and overcome in daily living. Above all, we should remember that Christ works through a believer's brokenness.

In the hospital I listened to my fellow patients and pointed them to the scripture that says, 'If we confess our sins, he is faithful and just to forgive us our sins, and cleanse us from all unrighteousness' (1 John 1:9, KJV). Christ died that we might be forgiven. I prayed for them individually, and interceded for the staff in my quiet times.

There are so many lovely promises in the Bible. The promise that sustained me, and that I clung to against all the odds when I was bereft of husband and children, home, family and friends, was 'We know that all things work together for good for those who love God, who are called according to his purpose' (Romans 8:28, NRSV). I did not know who or what I was, except that I was a Christian and that years earlier I had had a dream telling me to 'be a Barnabas'.

Later, when I was released from hospital and given back the children, I made Jacob's vow my own: 'If God will be with me, and will keep me in this way that I go, and will give me bread to eat and clothing to wear... then the Lord shall be my God... and of all that you give me I will surely give one tenth to you' (Genesis 28:20–22). It was some years before I fulfilled the full tithing, but God has never let me down.

Now I am a widow with five children and many grandchildren. It is said that we make God in the image of our parents—let that be a spur to those of us who have children, to try to be parents in the image of God. We need to read and read the Bible so that our minds are saturated with the holiness, majesty, justice and overwhelming kindness of God our Father. My children do not go to church but allow me to read Bible stories to their children.

We should also never forget that Jesus is the Word made flesh. God in his infinite love, generosity and wisdom became a human being—that wonderful man of Galilee who went about doing good. He was tempted as we are, yet remained without sin, and gives us his righteousness in exchange for our sin. Some undiscerning parents are like the Pharisees, teaching man-made rules as God's law but allowing behaviour that grieves the Holy Spirit. We need to read the whole Bible and find out what God really says, and about what he is silent.

If we read the book of Genesis, we see that things did not always go well in Isaac's family, but God's covenant promise brought good out of evil. God answers our prayerful longings and immediate concerns if we look, listen, wait hopefully and act trustingly. God knows all about us and still loves us. He knows the words before they are on our lips. He knows what we are thinking. He made us; he knows everything that has ever happened to us. He knows our parents' strengths and failings and how they have affected us. Neither we, our parents, nor anybody else is perfect, but God still loves us, just as we are, and pities our weaknesses and will help us as we live day by day.

We may find, for example, that anger wells up within us, and we can ask God to help us channel this anger in the right way. The word of God, sharper than any two-edged sword, may pierce us, convicting us of our sin, but then we can cry out for forgiveness and mercy, knowing that God will always hear us and wash our sin and guilt away.

Like Eve, in the garden of Eden, I have wanted to be wise! I read, 'If any of you is lacking in wisdom, ask God, who gives to all gener- ously and ungrudgingly, and it will be given you' (James 1:5), and I clung to that. God can give us a holy wisdom if we apply ourselves to learn the truths in the Bible and the principles they embrace, and which ones apply to our particular situation. We should soak our minds in scripture. Here is a suggestion: set yourself the task of read- ing the whole Bible. There are more than one attractively laid out versions of the Bible-in-a-year.

The New Living Bible edition is refreshing, with two chapters of the Old Testament, one of the New Testament, a Psalm and a Proverb daily, in a reading that takes ten or twelve minutes. The Church of England *Common Worship* service book also has an excel- lent lectionary (system of Bible readings) that takes you through much of the Bible over three years.

Whatever system you are guided to use, be sure that much prayer will have gone into the choosing of each day's passages. I am amazed how often the half-formed questions in my mind are answered in some part of the daily reading, and it is wonderful to start to see how all the truths of scripture are interrelated.

The book of Proverbs tells us that there is wisdom in many coun- sellors! Of course it is helpful to get advice from others, but we should remember that God will give us wisdom if we ask him for it. In Psalm 119, the longest psalm in the Bible, we read, 'Your [God's] commandment makes me wiser than my enemies, for it is always with me. I have more understanding than all my teachers, for your decrees are my meditation. I understand more than the aged, for I keep your precepts... Through your precepts I get understanding; therefore I hate every false way' (vv. 98–100, 104). In verse 103, the psalmist exclaims: 'How sweet are your words to my taste, sweeter than honey to my mouth!'

At one time I thought I needed only God and the Bible, but a very loving, though spiritually reticent church slowly taught me to see Christ in other people. At informal group Bible studies and prayer meetings in my home, I learned to hear God speaking through the love and wisdom of other Christians. I am so glad that they did not try to cast demons out of me—that would have been devastating. They just said, 'God loves you; God is in control' and were patient with me.

I am now living in a Christian community in sheltered housing and am back at my home church, where I was born again over fifty years ago, met my husband as a teenager soon after, and was married. I am learning more about prayer and that my dependence is upon Christ Jesus my Saviour and friend, seen in his servants of all brands of churchmanship. There is so much more to learn and experience, resting in the assurance that the Holy Spirit never guides contrary to scripture and we need 'every word that comes from the mouth of the Lord' (Deuteronomy 8:3).

Reading the Bible increases faith, not only faith in Christ but in the grace of God, by which I mean his overarching Fatherhood, and his infinite kindness to us individuals who believe in him. I want to end, therefore, by urging you to 'search the scriptures' daily. By doing so, you will find revealed our Saviour, the dear Lord Jesus Christ, crucified, dead, risen, ascended, glorified, and ever living now to make intercession for us.

An extract from
Song of the Shepherd

Of all the psalms written by King David, the most popular and well-known is Psalm 23, yet its very familiarity may lead us to miss its beauty and fail to hear its message. Song of the Shepherd *shows that the picture of the loving shepherd and his sheep speaks profoundly about how we can relate to God. Author Tony Horsfall examines the psalm verse by verse, covering key discipleship issues for both new and mature Christians—learning how to rest in God, how to trust him through difficult times, how to live from the resources he provides.*

The Lord is the Shepherd

Given the pastoral nature of life in ancient Israel, we should not be surprised to find that God uses imagery taken from this aspect of their everyday world to communicate with his people. By declaring himself to be their Shepherd, God was reaching deep into the psyche of the people of Israel, a people who from the very beginning of their existence had been pastoral nomads. The special relationship that exists between shepherd and sheep was well known to them: it was something they felt and knew instinctively. They were surrounded by living examples of the interaction between shepherd and sheep. The significance of God's self-revelation would not be lost on any of them.

Those of us living in the urban environment characteristic of the 21st century have to work a little harder at understanding and appreciating the pastoral imagery used in Psalm 23. Even for those of us who are more aware of rural life, and sheep farming in particular, there remains a gap in our understanding. We are not so intimately connected to pastoral life, and there are significant differences between shepherding in the ancient Near East and modern-day sheep farming as many of us observe it. Nevertheless, the scriptures are so full of shepherd–sheep imagery that we can quickly transport ourselves back into biblical times and use our imaginations to see what truths lie behind the metaphor.

Although David is credited with writing Psalm 23, the picture of God as a shepherd actually goes back much further in time to Jacob, one of the patriarchs of the nation of Israel. All the patriarchs kept flocks, and shepherding was part of their way of life, crucial to their survival. When the time comes to pray a blessing over his grandchildren (Joseph's sons, Ephraim and Manasseh), it is natural for Jacob to look back over his own life and pray to the covenant-keeping God who has been with him throughout—'the God who has been my shepherd all my life to this day' (Genesis 48:15).

Jacob's words describe how he perceived and understood his relationship to God. He saw himself in a personal relationship with a God who was leading and guiding him on life's journey, and who was gently watching over him in the way a shepherd would watch over his sheep. His life was not a random series of chance events or haphazard occurrences. No, there was meaning and purpose to it, because God was leading him. Looking back, he can see the Shepherd shaping the events of his turbulent life, and this is the same blessing that he now prays for his grandchildren.

The thought of God shepherding or leading his people occurs repeatedly throughout the Old Testament story. At no point in the history of Israel were the people more convinced of God's shepherding activity than during the exodus, that great event when Moses led them out of slavery in Egypt. It may have been only with hindsight that they could see it, but Israel's prophets always interpreted this great deliverance as a divine act—an intervention by the Shepherd of Israel.

The psalm writer Asaph, for instance, places this interpretation on those formative events: 'But [God] brought his people out like a flock; he led them like sheep through the desert. He guided them safely, so they were unafraid; but the sea engulfed their enemies' (Psalm 78:52–53). And again he says, 'You led your people like a flock by the hand of Moses and Aaron' (Psalm 77:20).

Asaph's understanding is of a God who is intimately involved with his people, leading and guiding them even through difficulties and dangers, and in the presence of their enemies. Some scholars see many echoes of the events of this period in Psalm 23. Indeed, if we read the passage with the exodus and wilderness wanderings in mind, it is not difficult to see that Israel's own history provides a suitable backdrop for David's writing.

Later prophets continued to see evidence of the shepherding activity of God on behalf of Israel. The period of the exile was a painful time of chastening for the nation, but God did not abandon them. Even there they could see his hand at work, and feel his shepherd's heart. Jeremiah looks forward to a day when Israel will return to her own land: 'He who scattered Israel will gather them and will watch over his flock like a shepherd' (Jeremiah 31:10). Again, 'I myself will gather the remnant of my flock out of all the countries where I have driven them and will bring them back to their pasture, where they will be fruitful and increase in number' (Jeremiah 23:3).

Isaiah, with the exile in mind, sees the Lord tenderly bringing the people back, sensitive to their needs, carefully leading them home like the good Shepherd he is: 'He tends his flock like a shepherd: he gathers the lambs in his arms and carries them close to his heart; he gently leads those that have young' (Isaiah 40:11).

Ezekiel contrasts the faithful care of God with that of the faithless leaders of Israel. God will not abandon his people at their moment of need, or think only of his own self-interest. 'I myself will search for my sheep and look after them. As a shepherd looks after his scattered flock when he is with them, so will I look after my sheep. I will rescue them from all the places where they were scattered on a day of clouds and darkness' (Ezekiel 34:11–12).

Whether in the exodus, or in the return from exile, the gracious activity of God can be seen. Israel did not deserve such care and attention. God responded to them from the grace within his own heart, and out of the covenant relationship that he had established with them, not because of any merit on their part. Not surprisingly, 'Shepherd of Israel' became a favourite name for God, and the inspiration behind many heartfelt cries for help at other times: 'Hear us, O Shepherd of Israel, you who lead Joseph like a flock... Awaken your might; come and save us' (Psalm 80:1–2).

What, then, can we say about a God who describes himself as a shepherd? What is he like, and what does he do? Everything in Psalm 23 is in keeping with the sheep-lore of the day, with 'good practice', as we would call it now. There is nothing that contradicts the real life of a shepherd with his sheep. This is why the psalm is best understood through the eyes of David's own experience as a shepherd.

Clearly a shepherd is a person with considerable skill and knowledge of his craft. It takes generations of understanding, handed down from one family member to another, to make a good shepherd, and years of personal experience out in the field before an individual really knows the sheep. Fortunately God has that kind of understanding of each of us because he made us and knows us individually. We are the sheep of his pasture and he knows us through and through.

A shepherd must be both brave and strong—strong because he is often alone in rugged and remote places, in all kinds of weather; and brave because he must protect his flock from wild animals and robbers. At the same time he must be tender and gentle—able to care for his flock, tending the ones that are sick or injured, helping those that are weak or lame. How blessed we are to have a God who is strong enough to help us in need, yet gentle enough to feel our pain and our hurt!

A shepherd must have a good heart, one that puts the needs of his flock above his own self-interest. He must not be harsh or brutal with the sheep, and must be willing to expose himself to danger in order to find any that have gone missing. Personal sacrifice is inevitable for a shepherd who truly cares for his flock. The character of God is such that, without hesitation, we would call him a good shepherd. Everything we know of him speaks of his commitment to us and his willingness to lay down his life for us.

Most importantly, the shepherd must be able to lead his flock, guiding them to find rich pasture and refreshing water. He is responsible to provide for them. He is their guide who goes before them, leading the way. The God we worship is a God who can be trusted. We can safely commit our lives to him and know that he will guide us in the right paths. With him as our leader we shall never go astray, and with him as our guide we shall lack for nothing.

So what does the shepherd do? He leads, he provides, he protects, he cares. And what is he like? He is skilful, brave, tender and wise. These are the activities and attributes of the Lord who is our Shepherd. With him by our side, we can be content.

To order a copy of this book, please turn to page 157.

An extract from
Transforming the Ordinary

Like John Henstridge's first book, Step into the Light
(BRF, 2000), Transforming the Ordinary *is a series of prayer
meditations based around Bible passages, helping us build
awareness of God into our daily routines. From celebrating a
birthday to being stuck in a queue of traffic, the thirty meditations
cover a range of familiar experiences and events, showing how we
can learn, whatever our circumstances, to tune our hearts and
minds into God's presence, there with us.*

I am blessed: I lift up my heart

Reflection / Discussion

There are moments in all our lives—however plain and simple or
even tedious—when we feel a sense of great joy and blessing, of
overwhelming happiness and contentment. Such moments may be
quite unexpected; we suddenly become aware of how wonderfully
blessed we are, how much we have to make us thankful.

Such moments may occur when we have our family around us
and we are pleased and grateful for them, for their love—brothers
and sisters, parents, children, grandparents, grandchildren, nephews
and nieces—they can bring such joy and happiness. We relax and
feel a great wealth of happiness in their company.

Or it may be a special occasion. You have won a prize and feel
rewarded for all your efforts; or you are being given praise for an
achievement, the completion of a good piece of work. Perhaps you
have performed well at music or sport, and have a sense of great satisfaction and fulfilment.

It may simply be at the end of a happy day—perhaps one of those blissful summer days when you can be outside, when you can't help feeling good, perhaps glowing, because of the warmth of the sun embracing you, and the world around is alive with colour and beauty. Perhaps you have a sense of peace and well-being. You could be on holiday, with time to unwind and reflect on your blessings.

These precious moments may come unexpectedly; and we might say to ourselves, 'I am so happy; I wish this could last for ever.' When are your moments of great happiness and contentment?

From the Bible (John 20:1–20)

After Jesus was so cruelly executed by the Romans, who were colluding with his enemies, he was buried in the tomb of a friend with as much honour and dignity as could be managed just before the sabbath began.

Early on the day after the sabbath, some women came to the tomb to finish the rituals of anointing.

To their amazement, the stone had been rolled away. Mary Magdalene ran to tell Peter and John, who in turn ran to the tomb. To their very great surprise, they found the tomb empty and, not yet understanding its significance, went back to the other disciples.

Meanwhile, Mary was in tears because she believed that someone had stolen the body. Blinded by her tears, she saw someone whom she took to be the gardener. The man asked her why she was crying; so Mary asked him if he knew where the body was.

Jesus just said her name: 'Mary!'

Her surprise and joy were beyond words. She fell at his feet saying, 'Rabbouni!' which means 'Master'.

Jesus told her not to cling to him, but to go and tell his followers, so she duly went and announced with great joy, 'I have seen the Lord!'

Meditation

Imagine that you are Mary Magdalene—a devoted follower of Jesus, to whom you owe so very much. In fact, you owe everything you are to him, for he has renewed your life.

You have been devastated by the cruel end to his life, the treachery that led to his capture, the mockery of a trial, and the torture and crucifixion. You are totally heartbroken, in despair.

After the rather hasty burial on the eve of the sabbath, you get up at first light the morning after the sabbath to complete the burial rituals—a loving duty.

You get to the tomb. Imagine your surprise to find that the great stone at the opening of the tomb has been rolled to one side. How, you wonder, could that have happened?

Perhaps you had better tell the others.

You run back into the town to tell Peter, who, with John, immediately runs to the tomb. When they get there, you are shocked to discover that the body has been taken away. Who could have done such a thing?

You are desperately upset, and in floods of tears—bitter tears. After all that has happened, how can this be?

There are angels in the tomb—a vision, perhaps? You are in such a state that you hardly know what is happening. 'Why are you crying?' one of them asks.

'They have taken away my Lord', you reply, 'and I do not know where he is'.

As you turn in the doorway, you see someone—the gardener—and he asks the same question: 'Why are you crying?'

Maybe he knows what they have done with the body. 'If you know,' you say, 'tell me where he is.'

The reply is just one word: 'Mary!' That voice—you know that voice. It is the Lord!

You fall at his feet, saying, 'Master!'

What joy this is. He tells you not to hold on to him, but to go on and tell the others that he is risen.

Wonderful joy overwhelms you. What marvellous blessing—to be the first to meet the Lord risen from the dead. It's a moment of sheer delight, which you would like to last for ever.

Now think of a present day moment of joy and blessing. In your imagination, try to picture yourself in that time of great happiness.

Picture the scene and the people around you as you bask in the wonderful sense of being blessed.

Now bring into that scene the same sense of joy and happiness that you felt as Mary when you met and recognized the risen Christ.

You bring Jesus, the risen Lord, into the present moment of blessedness.

The glorious resurrection of the Lord Jesus comes into our hearts and minds in the earthly and present moment of joy. We think of him here and now—his glorious presence, his wonderful victory over sin and death.

Jesus is real, Jesus is truly alive. He is here sharing this moment of bliss.

How good it is to be alive. How good it is to be here at this time and on this day. How overwhelming the sense of wonder and joy and new life.

Jesus is here and we hear his words, 'Peace be with you.' We let his joy and peace soak into our hearts as we and the risen Christ share this moment of joy and contentment, of uplifted spirits.

Our hearts are full of gladness as we give you thanks and praise, Lord, for your wonderful and generous presence. Glory be to you, O Lord, for all the moments of blessing we experience in your world.

To order a copy of this book, please turn to page 157.

Recommended reading

Growing Leaders
by James Lawrence

In some church circles it is not unusual to be suspicious of the application of 'business ideas' in what is deemed an exclusively 'spiritual' area—Christian leadership. After all, if the minister is sincere and prays a lot, surely s/he will manage the job without resorting to 'secular' jargon and techniques, as ministers have done down the centuries?

Growing Leaders paints a stark picture by way of an answer: seven out of ten Christian leaders today feel heavily overworked, four in ten suffer financial pressures, while only two in ten have had training in management or team building. A sobering total of 1,500 give up their job over a ten-year period. At the same time, as financial restrictions affect the availability of full-time ministers, more people are needed for leadership roles in local congregations, in every area of church work.

As well as presenting the bad news, though, *Growing Leaders* faces head-on the challenge of raising up new leaders and also helping existing leaders to develop and mature as they continue in their roles. It uses the model for growing leaders at the heart of the Arrow Leadership Programme, a ministry of the Church Pastoral Aid Society (CPAS), which is managed by the book's author, James Lawrence.

James is an ordained minister in the Church of England and has spent time in parish ministry as well as being a member of Springboard, the Archbishops' initiative on evangelism. *Growing Leaders* is his second book for BRF: he has also written *Lost for Words* (BRF, 1999) and *Men: the Challenge of Change* (CPAS, 1997).

This new book reflects the breadth of his research into leadership. He also shares honestly some of his personal experiences—both positive and negative—in leadership situations, while noting the importance of acknowledging different personality types. What may work well for him could be the worst approach for somebody else.

One of the book's major themes is how the key to fruitful leadership lies in awareness of the dangers of living in the 'red zone' of stress. James shows that, sadly, this is an all-too-common state of being for leaders, and he argues passionately for recognizing and then changing the factors that drive so many to burnout and even total breakdown. Instead of being driven by forces within ourselves that we have never admitted, let alone understood, we can learn to make wise choices and develop a rhythm of life that holds in balance work, leisure, friendship and family.

The book is clearly structured, with section headings that spell out the overall message: Growing leaders know they're chosen, discern God's call, develop Christ-like character, cultivate competence, and lead in community. A concluding resources section offers in-depth exploration of six themes mentioned more briefly elsewhere, from 'discerning your spiritual gifts' to 'guidelines for establishing a mentoring relationship'.

What impressed me most about *Growing Leaders*, however, is how it combines comprehensive analysis of good leadership skills with a stress on Christian discipleship. Building a close relationship with God is shown as central to true leadership competence, more foundational than the most insightful technique of secular management theory.

The book surveys relevant Bible passages to show how God can choose to call the most unlikely people to leadership, and that travelling the path of discipleship may involve discerning and then following that calling in obedience ourselves. Furthermore, those who are called to leadership are also called to train up others as leaders. Some of the book's most thought-provoking sections argue for the crucial importance of team building, rather than the traditional 'lonely prophet on a mountain-top' style of leadership.

This is not a book for full-time ministers only. It is for anybody who exercises a leadership role (or who thinks they may be called to such a role) in either a church congregation or Christian organization. Another of the strengths of *Growing Leaders* is the way it demonstrates how many of the skills needed to lead a small Bible study group apply equally to leading a large team of co-workers in an office environment.

The awesome responsibility of leadership is summed up in the heading of the book's tenth chapter: 'Leaders discern, articulate and implement God's vision'. It inspires leaders (and potential leaders) with the scope of their calling, while offering enough good advice and plain common sense to avoid any sense of being daunted by the task ahead.

Naomi Starkey, Commissioning Editor for BRF's Adult List

For reflection

Confessions *by Augustine of Hippo*

'Great are you, O Lord, and greatly to be praised; great is your power, and infinite is your wisdom.' And man desires to praise you, for he is a part of your creation; he bears his mortality about with him and carries the evidence of his sin and the proof that you resist the proud. Still he desires to praise you, this man who is only a small part of your creation. You have prompted him, that he should delight to praise you, for you have made us for yourself and restless is our heart until it comes to rest in you.

Grant me, O Lord, to know and understand whether first to invoke you or to praise you; whether first to know you or call upon you. But who can invoke you, knowing you not? For he who knows you not may invoke you as another than you are. It may be that we should invoke you in order that we may come to know you. But 'how shall they call on him in whom they have not believed? Or how shall they believe without a preacher?' Now, 'they shall praise the Lord who seek him,' for 'those who seek shall find him,' and, finding him, shall praise him. I will seek you, O Lord, and call upon you. I call upon you, O Lord, in my faith which you have given me, which you have inspired in me through the humanity of your Son, and through the ministry of your preacher.

And how shall I call upon my God—my God and my Lord? For when I call on him I ask him to come into me. And what place is there in me into which my God can come? How could God, the God who made both heaven and earth, come into me? Is there anything in me, O Lord my God, that can contain you? Do even the heaven and the earth, which you have made, and in which you did make me, contain you? Is it possible that, since without you nothing would be which does exist, you made it so that whatever exists has some capacity to receive you? Why, then, do I ask you to come into me, since I also am and could not be if you were not in me? For I am not, after all, in hell—and yet you are there too, for 'if I go down into hell, you are there'. Therefore I would not exist—I would simply not be at all—unless I exist in you, from whom and by whom and in whom all things are... Where, beyond heaven and earth, could I go that there my God might come to me—he who has said, 'I fill heaven and earth'?

Since, then, you fill the heaven and earth, do they contain you? Or, do you fill and overflow them, because they cannot contain you? And where do you pour out what remains of you after heaven and earth are full? ... the vessels which you fill do not confine you, since even if they were broken, you would not be poured out. And, when you are poured out on us, you are not thereby brought down; rather, we are uplifted. You are not scattered; rather, you gather us together. But when you fill all things, do you fill them with your whole being? Or, since not even all things together could contain you altogether, does any one thing contain a single part, and do all things contain that same part at the same time? Do singulars contain you singly? Do greater things contain more of you, and smaller things less? Or, is it not rather that you are wholly present everywhere, yet in such a way that nothing contains you wholly?

What, therefore, is my God? ... Most high, most excellent, most potent, most omnipotent; most merciful and most just; most secret and most truly present; most beautiful and most strong; stable, yet not supported; unchangeable, yet changing all things; never new, never old; making all things new, yet bringing old age upon the proud, and they know it not; always working, ever at rest; gathering, yet needing nothing; sustaining, pervading, and protecting; creating, nourishing, and developing; seeking, and yet possessing all things. You love, but without passion; are jealous, yet free from care; repent without remorse; angry, yet remaining serene. You change your ways, leaving your plans unchanged; you recover what you have never really lost. You are never in need but still you rejoice at your gains; are never greedy, yet demand dividends... Yet, O my God, my life, my holy Joy, what is this that I have said? What can any man say when he speaks of you? But woe to them that keep silence—since even those who say most are dumb.

Augustine of Hippo (345–430), From Confessions, *Book 1, chapters 1—4*

Other Christina Press titles

Who'd Plant a Church? Diana Archer
£5.99 in UK
Planting an Anglican church from scratch, with a team of four—
two adults and two children—is an unusual adventure even in
these days. Diana Archer is a vicar's wife who gives a distinctive
perspective on parish life.

Pathway Through Grief edited by Jean Watson
£6.99 in UK
Ten Christians, each bereaved, share their experience of loss.
Frank and sensitive accounts offering comfort and reassurance
to those recently bereaved. Jean Watson has lost her own husband and believes that those involved in counselling will also
gain new insights from these honest personal chronicles.

God's Catalyst Rosemary Green
£8.99 in UK
Rosemary Green's international counselling ministry has prayer
and listening to God at its heart. Changed lives and rekindled
faith testify to God's healing power. Here she provides insight,
inspiration and advice for both counsellors and concerned
Christians who long to be channels of God's Spirit to help those
in need. *God's Catalyst* is a unique tool for the non-specialist
counsellor; for the pastor who has no training; for the Christian
who wants to come alongside hurting friends.

Angels Keep Watch Carol Hathorne
£5.99 in UK
A true adventure showing how God still directs our lives, not
with wind, earthquake or fire, but by the still, small voice.
  'Go to Africa.' The Lord had been saying it for over forty
years. At last, Carol Hathorne had obeyed, going out to Kenya
with her husband. On the eastern side of Nairobi, where tourists
never go, they came face to face with dangers, hardships and
poverty on a daily basis, but experienced the joy of learning that
Christianity is still growing in God's world.

Not a Super-Saint Liz Hansford
£6.99 in UK

'You might have thought Adrian Plass… had cornered the market in amusing diary writing. Well, check out Liz Hansford's often hilarious account of life as a Baptist minister's wife in Belfast. Highly recommended.' *The New Christian Herald*

Liz Hansford describes the outlandish situations which arise in the Manse, where life is both fraught and tremendous fun. *Not a Super-Saint* is for the ordinary Christian who feels they must be the only one who hasn't quite got it all together.

The Addiction of a Busy Life Edward England
£5.99 in UK

Twelve lessons from a devastating heart attack. Edward, a giant of Christian publishing in the UK, and founder of Christina Press, shares what the Lord taught him when his life nearly came to an abrupt end. Although not strictly a Christina title (Edward lacks the gender qualifications), we believe you may want to buy this for the busy men in your lives.

'A wonderful story of success and frailty, of love and suffering, of despair and hope. If you are too busy to read this book, you are too busy.' *Dr Michael Green*

Life Path Luci Shaw
£5.99 in UK

Personal and spiritual growth through journal writing. Life has a way of slipping out of the back door while we're not looking. Keeping a journal can enrich life as we live it, and bring it all back later. Luci Shaw shows how a journal can also help us grow in our walk with God.

Precious to God Sarah Bowen
£5.99 in UK

Two young people, delighted to be starting a family, have their expectations shattered by the arrival of a handicapped child. And yet this is only the first of many difficulties to be faced. What was initially a tragedy is, through faith, transformed into a story of inspiration, hope and spiritual enrichment.

All the above titles are available from Christian bookshops everywhere, or in case of difficulty, direct from Christina Press using the order form on page 156.

Other BRF titles

Growing Leaders James Lawrence
Reflections on leadership, life and Jesus
£7.99 in UK
Seven out of ten Christian leaders feel overworked, four in ten
suffer financial pressures, only two in ten have had management
training, and 1,500 give up their job over a ten-year period. At
the same time, as financial restrictions affect the availability of
full-time ministers, more people are needed for leadership roles
in local congregations, for every area of church work.

This book faces the challenge of raising up new leaders and
helping existing leaders to mature, using the model for growing
leaders at the heart of the Arrow Leadership Programme, a
ministry of the Church Pastoral Aid Society (CPAS). It com-
prehensively surveys leadership skills and styles, discerning our
personal calling, avoiding the 'red zone' of stress, developing
character, and living as part of the community of God's people.

Why Siblings Matter Anna Brooker
Growing strong relationships in church and community
£6.99 in UK
For people of all ages today, life can feel fickle. One day the
scene seems happy and secure, the next all security is washed
away as unresolved tensions, hurts and differences add to the
everyday pressures of life. What do we cling on to at such times
—friends, relatives, collegues, the church?

This book looks at the importance of sibling relationships
in our individual lives and in families. It considers how these
horizontal relationships can strengthen families as much as the
vertical, parent–child relationships can. It also looks at the biblical principles that may be applied to practical issues in order to
withstand the external and internal pressures of today's world.

Easy Ways to Seasonal Fun for the Very Young Vicki Howie
Twelve Bible-based activities for 3–5s
£9.99 in UK
From January to December there is something for every season in this comprehensive teaching book for very young children. *Seasonal Fun for the Very Young* provides the perfect complement to Vicki Howie's popular title, *Bible Fun for the Very Young*. Once again, Vicki offers twelve simple, off-the-peg sessions for those working with the 3–5s in primary education or church-based pre-school groups.

Each session uses strong visual aids for the single-focus teaching point, well within the exprience of young children and appropriately introduced through Teddy and the story basket. The twelve sessions give a wealth of ideas for every season of the year, including Advent, Christmas, Epiphany, Candlemas, Mothering Sunday, Palm Sunday, Easter, Pentecost, a teddy bears' picnic and a pram service for the summer, Harvest and All Saints' Day.

The Lord's Prayer Unplugged Lucy Moore
A wealth of ideas opening up the prayer in ten sessions
£12.99 in UK
The Lord's Prayer Unplugged provides a unique opportunity to explore the biblical breadth and depth encapsulated in Jesus' famous prayer. The material can be used as a complete teaching programme over the course of ten weeks.

Alternatively, each unit stands alone so that the phrases can be studied separately and linked into the teaching of a Bible passage springing from the phrase. An index of Bible passages is included at the end of the book.

Each phrase of the prayer is explored through creative ideas, offering a wealth of thematic gems for teachers to pick and choose to suit their situation.

All the above titles are available from Christian bookshops everywhere or, in case of difficulty, direct from BRF using the order form on page 157.

Christina Press Publications Order Form

All of these publications are available from Christian bookshops everywhere or, in case of difficulty, direct from the publisher. Please make your selection below, complete the payment details and send your order with payment as appropriate to:

Christina Press Ltd, 17 Church Road, Tunbridge Wells, Kent TN1 1LG

		Qty	Price	Total
8700	God's Catalyst	____	£8.99	____
8702	Precious to God	____	£5.99	____
8703	Angels Keep Watch	____	£5.99	____
8704	Life Path	____	£5.99	____
8705	Pathway Through Grief	____	£6.99	____
8706	Who'd Plant a Church?	____	£5.99	____
8708	Not a Super-Saint	____	£6.99	____
8705	The Addiction of a Busy Life	____	£5.99	____

POSTAGE AND PACKING CHARGES				
	UK	Europe	Surface	Air Mail
£7.00 & under	£1.25	£2.25	£2.25	£3.50
£7.10–£29.99	£2.25	£5.50	£7.50	£11.00
£30.00 & over	free	prices on request		

Total cost of books £ ____
Postage and Packing £ ____
TOTAL £ ____

All prices are correct at time of going to press, are subject to the prevailing rate of VAT and may be subject to change without prior warning.

Name _____

Address _____

_____

_____ Postcode _____

Total enclosed £ _____ (cheques should be made payable to 'Christina Press Ltd')

☐ Please send me further information about Christina Press publications

BRF Publications Order Form

All of these publications are available from Christian bookshops everywhere, or in case of difficulty direct from the publisher. Please make your selection below, complete the payment details and send your order with payment as appropriate to:

BRF, First Floor, Elsfield Hall, 15–17 Elsfield Way, Oxford OX2 8FG

			Qty	Price	Total
316 1	Transforming the Ordinary		____	£6.99	____
291 2	Song of the Shepherd		____	£6.99	____
246 7	Growing Leaders		____	£7.99	____
260 2	Why Siblings Matter		____	£6.99	____
342 0	Seasonal Fun for the Very Young		____	£9.99	____
262 9	The Lord's Prayer Unplugged		____	£12.99	____

POSTAGE AND PACKING CHARGES				
	UK	Europe	Surface	Air Mail
£7.00 & under	£1.25	£3.00	£3.50	£5.50
£7.10–£29.99	£2.25	£5.50	£6.50	£10.00
£30.00 & over	free	prices on request		

Total cost of books   £ _____

Postage and Packing   £ _____

TOTAL   £ _____

All prices are correct at time of going to press, are subject to the prevailing rate of VAT and may be subject to change without prior warning.

Name _____

Address _____

_____

_____ Postcode _____

Total enclosed £ _____ (cheques should be made payable to 'BRF')

Payment by: cheque ❏ postal order ❏ Visa ❏ Mastercard ❏ Switch ❏

Card no. ⬚⬚⬚⬚⬚⬚⬚⬚⬚⬚⬚⬚⬚⬚⬚⬚

Card expiry date ⬚⬚⬚⬚   Issue number (Switch) ⬚⬚⬚⬚

Signature _____

(essential if paying by credit/Switch card)

❏ Please do not send me further information about BRF publications

Visit the BRF website at www.brf.org.uk

DBDWG0204

BRF is a Registered Charity

Subscription Information

Each issue of *Day by Day with God* is available from Christian book-shops everywhere. Copies may also be available through your church Book Agent or from the person who distributes Bible reading notes in your church.

Alternatively you may obtain *Day by Day with God* on subscription direct from the publishers. There are two kinds of subscription:

Individual Subscriptions are for four copies or less, and include postage and packing. To order an annual Individual Subscription please complete the details on page 160 and send the coupon with payment to BRF in Oxford. You can also use the form to order a Gift Subscription for a friend.

Church Subscriptions are for five copies or more, sent to one address, and are supplied post free. Church Subscriptions run from 1 May to 30 April each year and are invoiced annually. To order a Church Subscription please complete the details opposite and send the coupon to BRF in Oxford. You will receive an invoice with the first issue of notes.

All subscription enquiries should be directed to:

BRF
First Floor
Elsfield Hall
15–17 Elsfield Way
Oxford
OX2 8FG

Tel: 01865 319700
Fax: 01865 319701
E-mail: subscriptions@brf.org.uk
Website: www.brf.org.uk

Day by Day with God is also available from your local Christian bookshop.

Church Subscriptions

The Church Subscription rate for *Day by Day with God* will be £10.50 per person until April 2005.

❏ I would like to take out a church subscription for _____ (Qty) copies.

❏ Please start my order with the September 2004/January/May 2005* issue.

I would like to pay annually/receive an invoice with each edition of the notes*.

(*Please delete as appropriate)

Please do not send any money with your order. Send your order to BRF and we will send you an invoice. The Church Subscription year is from May to April. If you start subscribing in the middle of a subscription year we will invoice you for the remaining number of issues left in that year.

Name and address of the person organising the Church Subscription:

Name _____

Address _____

_____

Postcode _____ Telephone _____

Church _____

Name of Minister _____

Name and address of the person paying the invoice if the invoice needs to be sent directly to them:

Name _____

Address _____

_____

Postcode _____ Telephone _____

Please send your coupon to:

BRF
First Floor
Elsfield Hall
15–17 Elsfield Way
Oxford
OX2 8FG

❏ Please do not send me further information about BRF publications

DBDWG0204   BRF is a Registered Charity

Individual Subscriptions

❏ I would like to give a gift subscription (please complete both name and address sections below)

❏ I would like to take out a subscription myself (complete name and address details only once)

The completed coupon should be sent with appropriate payment to BRF. Alternatively, please write to us quoting your name, address, the subscription you would like for either yourself or a friend (with their name and address), the start date and credit card number, expiry date and signature if paying by credit card.

Gift subscription name _____

Gift subscription address _____

_____

_____ Postcode _____

Please send to the above for one year, beginning with the September 2004/January/ May 2005 issue: (delete as applicable)

	UK	Surface	Air Mail
Day by Day with God	❏ £12.45	❏ £13.80	❏ £16.05
2-year subscription	❏ £21.90	N/A	N/A

Please complete the payment details below and send your coupon, with appropriate payment, to BRF, First Floor, Elsfield Hall, 15–17 Elsfield Way, Oxford OX2 8FG

Your name _____

Your address _____

_____

_____ Postcode _____

Total enclosed £ _____ (cheques should be made payable to 'BRF')

Payment by: cheque ❏ postal order ❏ Visa ❏ Mastercard ❏ Switch ❏

Card no. ☐☐☐☐☐☐☐☐☐☐☐☐☐☐☐☐☐☐

Card expiry date ☐☐☐☐   Issue number (Switch) ☐☐☐☐

Signature _____

(essential if paying by credit/Switch card)

NB: These notes are also available from Christian bookshops everywhere.

❏ Please do not send me further information about BRF publications

DBDWG0204   BRF is a Registered Charity